Window Music

Window Music

Letting in the Light

JUDY POLLARD SMITH

RESOURCE *Publications* · Eugene, Oregon

WINDOW MUSIC
Letting in the Light

Copyright © 2026 Judy Pollard Smith. All rights reserved. Except for brief quotations in critical publications or reviews, no part of this book may be reproduced in any manner without prior written permission from the publisher. Write: Permissions, Wipf and Stock Publishers, 199 W. 8th Ave., Suite 3, Eugene, OR 97401.

Resource Publications
An Imprint of Wipf and Stock Publishers
199 W. 8th Ave., Suite 3
Eugene, OR 97401

www.wipfandstock.com

PAPERBACK ISBN: 979-8-3852-6586-2
HARDCOVER ISBN: 979-8-3852-6587-9
EBOOK ISBN: 979-8-3852-6588-6

01/28/26

These thoughts are written with love for
Edwina and Hamish Post and Charlotte and Lucia Smith
that you keep growing towards the Light.
Your grandfather would be proud of you.

Contents

Preface | ix
Acknowledgments | xi
Prologue | xiii

Fiat Lux: Let There Be Light | 1
Leaning In | 6
Dusk, Twilight, Dark: Winter Evenings or Summer Evenings? | 9
Marginalia | 12
Diane's Paintbox | 15
Window Music | 17
The Moon and Me | 19
The Rach 3 Introduces the Sun | 22
The First Day of Spring | 23
Forgiven | 26
The Garden, the Sunshine, the Book | 28
Back Porch, Special Glasses, the Eclipse | 31
A Little Window Music at Noon | 32
My Old Table, My Dining Room Chair, My Mug That Holds the Pens | 33
Mrs. Fithian | 36
Today | 39
Outside Spaces and Inside Places | 41

CONTENTS

Bright and Beautiful | 44
Into the Light | 46
The Literary Salon and How to Have One | 48
The Intersection of Light and Love | 51
A World of Light | 54
A Little Window Music, Continued | 56
En Route | 57
Fellows of the Royal Society | 58
Sunday-ness | 61
A Little More Window Music | 64
Flowers | 65
The More, the Merrier | 68
Summertime | 71
Surge, Illuminare | 73
Canada Day: True Patriot Love | 76
A Little More Window Music | 79
The Dam Seed Catalogue | 81
The Light in the Story of the Picture in the Frame | 84
Utter, Lovely, Chaos | 87
The Dwindling of the Light | 90
The Front Lawn, the Neighbors, the Little Library | 92
Nighttime Windows | 95

Bibliography | 99

Preface

It takes courage to put one's thoughts on paper for all the world to see. In my case, it's not for all the world, but for anyone who happens across this small book of essays.

I have been writing since I was eight years old. I couldn't put the pencil down. Next it was the pen, followed by an old typewriter I found for half price when our three children were tiny. Now it's the laptop. If I had to vote, I might still choose the pen.

By the time the children were in their early teens, I was writing on occasion for the Personal Essay column in Canada's *Globe and Mail* newspaper and occasionally for the *National Post*, followed by book reviews for the *Hamilton Spectator*. Then it was short stories for literary magazines and for a British women's magazine. What great fun it was being paid in pounds sterling! I joined the Society of Women Writers and Journalists in Britain and won their silver Rosebowl award one year for a *Globe and Mail* essay. The rosebowl lives in Jane Austen's home, Chawton House, in the library.

I made myself a writer because I knew that nobody else would do it for me. At a writer's workshop, the advice was to write about what I know. So I do.

More recently, I published three books on varied themes. One was a true story using the vehicle of historical fiction about a young British woman who walked into King Leopold's Congo

PREFACE

and changed it politically, and with love, and she did it because she cared.

Another book was my year-long journal about aging because I'm curious to track how that works. The last book consists of a few essays which I dedicated to my late husband, whom I loved from the moment he invited me out for lunch, because when I said I was too tied up with work, he replied, "I can be there in fifteen minutes." He had me with that line.

So now we have this new, small book of short essays and thoughts.

I wrote them on my annoying laptop in the bright window in what I call the back room. I wrote them around the topic of light and how we welcome it into our lives. What are our sources? What do we depend upon to get us through? Friends? Family? Nature? Hobbies? Faith?

We could all do with a good dose of positivity, not false hope, but a look towards something more powerful than ourselves.

Thank you for taking the time to see what you think.

I can be reached at judypollardsmith@gmail.com.

I'd love to hear your own thoughts about light.

Acknowledgments

THIS WILL BE A more informative read if you choose a search engine to find and identify the paintings online. It is the significantly placed streams of light in these paintings that informed my thoughts and my words.

With my grateful thanks to Thomas Power, who encouraged, edited and gifted me the book that resulted in this one. Thank you, Meg Farrell Patterson, for your excellent formatting and for thinking of the word "dwindling" when I was stuck.

To Diane Wile-Brumm in Halifax, Nova Scotia, for her light-fueled cover painting, which began life on an easel, then became a postcard, and now is the cover for this book of thoughts. You will recognize it in a small essay inside.

To Hilary Brown Bierman, who, as a former CBC/ABC television journalist, stayed close by our side during the evacuation of Vietnam and resurfaced years later with new Syrian friends to share, author of *War Tourist, Memoirs of a Foreign Correspondent* (Friesen Press, 2021).

To Bernadette Rule, Canadian writer and poet, who published my short story when she was editor of *In The Wings, Stories of Forgotten Women*, which led to a much bigger story for me to unravel.

Further thanks to The Royal Society of Literature in England for allowing me to reuse the two short pieces included here that they published during the pandemic in their series, *Only Connect*.

ACKNOWLEDGMENTS

Thank you to the *Globe and Mail* newspaper for permitting me to reuse my essay from February 5, 2024. I have amended it.

Thank you to the *National Post* newspaper for allowing me to reuse much of the information in my essay, "The Key to Edith Wharton's Garden Kingdom," from April 4, 2014. It has been amended.

And thank you to Barbara Bos in Galacia, owner/editor of *Books by Women*, for allowing me to reuse my essay on literary salons from March 2015.

And to Hamiltonians Paul Lisson and Fiona Kinsella, thank you for allowing me permission to reuse my essay on The Seed Company from the *Hamilton Arts & Letters Magazine*.

Prologue

Light.
Where do we find it?
How do we incorporate it?
Light takes both form and function.
It comes to us from the sun, the moon, the stars.
It arrives with electricity, from fire, as the reflection in a mirror.
It peeks through clouds, shines through the arc of rainbows.
It nourishes all of life. It lightens our paths in both our days and our nights.
We cannot survive without it.
The following words speak of how light comes to me.

Fiat Lux
Let There Be Light

A conversation with the book *In Quiet Light: Poems on Vermeer's Women,* by Marilyn Chandler McEntyre.

WHEN I HOLD THIS book of some of my favorite paintings in my hand, my friend Marlene is right beside me. My fingers turn the pages that she turned. I consider the light coming from those Dutch windows that she considered, and maybe she thought the same thoughts that I'm thinking. It makes each page special to know that she was there before me. In her introduction to the book, the author-poet Marilyn Chandler McEntyre says that "these women articulate a rich respect for and understanding of womanliness." The artist "has honoured the image of God in womanly form," she further claims. Without ever having known Marlene, she has described her.

Something in ourselves is jolted awake when a work of art, either visual, poetic or literary, speaks aloud to us. We have an epiphany that cannot be quieted until we address it in some form. The first time I saw Vermeer's paintings, I was twenty-one years old on a visit to Amsterdam. I knew they were special.[1]

---

1. McEntyre, *In Quiet Light*, 20–22.

THE MILKMAID

The poet tells us that this serious, well-rounded young woman is "full of grace." She is a hard worker. We can see the evidence in the large loaf of heavily grained bread she has baked and laid on the table, maybe to be consumed by farm help. Her arms are heavily muscled. We can see her strength as she pours the milk from the heavy stone crockery jug. She is serious about her work. What is her life all about, we ask ourselves? Is she a farmer's wife? A mother? A hired cook?

The author-poet says that "her world is grained and gritty. . .simple and crude." We can assume then that this is not her house nor her belongings. There are no silk gowns in this portrait. No outward signs of wealth or privilege. What the viewer sees is a dedicated carer for those who depend upon her. To my mind, she is not a questioner, but a responder to other people's questions. She does what is expected of her.

A beam of light for which Vermeer is famous comes through the windowpane, lands on her kindly face, on her strong arms, on the crusted grain loaf her hands have prepared for others to eat.

"Full of grace" indeed.

GIRL WITH A PEARL EARRING

Perhaps *Girl With a Pearl Earring* is Vermeer's most famous work. She appears on page 25 of McEntyre's book. She is the milkmaid's opposite, for in her I see wealth, privilege, the famous earring itself, her lightly colored lips, the slim face, the blue silk headdress tied with elegance. Even on the earring, there is a tiny beam of light, seemingly showcasing her ability to own such an item. The poet McIntyre says she is "wrapped in light that fits her like her scarves . . ." and further refers to her as being "self-possessed." I think about the Milkmaid in the other painting I have just described who I imagine is also self-possessed, each of these two women inside of their own understanding. I look at the girl with the pearl earring, and I wonder if she knows how to make that loaf of bread.

WOMAN IN BLUE

Who owns this story?[2]

    I ask myself that question because in it I can see my own mother, who was expecting her first child while her husband went off to fight a war that was expected to be over in short order, not the five years it took for his return. Although the artist must have known his subject, I have adopted the subject as mine. I cannot help it. She has a letter in her hand, which, in my imagination, is from 'the front' as they call the war zones in Europe. She is not merely holding the letter in her hands; she has grasped it in a most unusual way to hold mere paper. She needs to take possession of each nuance, of his every word. It is all she has of him at this moment, the letter and their child who is growing in the swell of her blue-clad belly, the child who, with a hopeful blessing, the soldier-father-husband will come home to, to know and to love after Peace is declared. The light lands on her belly, focuses on it, takes care of the precious contents that float in the waters of life inside her. It is a lonely painting, the light from the window the only source of solace. In the actual painting, the poet-author imagines that the letter is from her husband, who is at sea. She wonders at the extent of the woman's ability to "bear the weight of all this love."

YOUNG WOMAN WITH A WATER PITCHER

She wears the snowy whiteness of a wide shoulder covering that includes her veiled head. Her clothing resembles that of a nun. But the golden threads of her waistcoat deny that occupation. She is a well-dressed young woman of some privilege.[3]

    She opens the window with her right hand, her left on a brass jug that perhaps contains water. She may be planning to open the window and throw the water on the tulips beneath. What we do know is that she is not poor, nor is she idle, and her calm, pretty

---

2. McEntyre, *In Quiet Light*, 27.
3. McEntyre, *In Quiet Light*, 35.

face does not look lonely. She appears satisfied with her life as she carries on her morning routines.

The window pours out a blessing of light onto the white headdress. The poet compares her to an acolyte and praises the light that "illumines" her.

THE GIRL WITH THE RED HAT

I chose to focus on this painting for two reasons.[4]

I was drawn to the Vermeer portrait immediately because the young woman has a startled look on her face, a non-compliant look. I wondered what the author-poet thought about it.

And I have, over my writing desk, a framed postcard from the Kelvingrove Museum in Glasgow, a portrait titled *The Lady with a Red Hat*, which is of Vita Sackville-West of writing fame, of Bloomsbury fame, of Sissinghurst garden fame. It was painted by Robert Strang, the Scottish portrait painter. The Vermeer painting and the similarly named Strang drew me to thinking about these two women, given that the titles of the paintings are similar. From what I know of the life of Vita Sackville-West and from what I gather of the women in the Vermeer painting just by looking at it, I'd guess that they had nothing in common at all except they both wore wide-brimmed red hats as they sat for their portraits. In the Strang portrait, Vita's shoulder turns to the right, but she turns her head to the artist full on. She stares boldly and unabashed into the light that falls on her face, but that covers one eye in shade. Her character in life was bold, out there, remarked upon, and so the artist captured her.

The Vermeer painting has the woman looking timidly into the light, a look of puzzlement on her face. It's as if she isn't sure why she is sitting there as his subject. She looks uncertain. Did she agree to this, or was this someone else's idea? She wants to run away and get it over with. Her expression says, "Get me out of here! Let me take off this ridiculous hat!" The poet has her say, "It's only

---

4. McEntyre, *In Quiet Light*, 59.

duty. I'd rather be washing linens in the sun, strolling by the canal, my hair loose in the wind . . ."

When she is finished with this nonsense, she plans to drop the hat into the canal and "watch it float away."

Ms. Sackville-West was a good writer, and I am glad I have her portrait over my desk, but that's where it ends for the two of us. I'm for the Vermeer girl and throwing the big, red hat into the canal.

Leaning In

"We write to taste life twice"

ANAIS NIN

I LEARN NEW THINGS every day, things that I have taken for granted and ideas I have previously been too preoccupied to entertain. In her inspiring book about Montaigne, *How to Live: Or a Life of Montaigne in One Question and Twenty Attempts at an Answer*, author Sarah Bakewell points out that as Montaigne grew older, "his desire to pay astounded attention to life did not decline; it intensified."

Montaigne lived from 1533 to 1592. He was a foremost French Renaissance philosopher. He popularized the idea of the essay as literature.

Ms. Bakewell writes that his outlook on aging was "to maintain a kind of naive amazement at each instant of experience," but as Montaigne learned, one of the best techniques for doing this is to write about everything. Simply describing an object on your table, or the view from your window, opens your eyes to how marvelous such ordinary things are."[1]

---

1. Bakewell, *How to Live*, 37, 38.

I've been trying to remember to take his wisdom unto myself, some of it due to the Japanese credo of 'forest bathing,' or *shinrin-yoku*. It affects the way I walk in nature. I don't just stroll. I look at everything beneath my feet and beside me and overhead. There might be a bird I miss, like the hawk in a nearby tree I spotted not too long ago.

Life is too big, too generous, to allow it to swim by without our noticing the small things, the tiny, wee things that have significance we don't slow down to marvel at, things like the Spring Peeper I saw at the Botanical Garden. It was an inch long and camouflaged to match the beige of the earth. The volunteer told me that if I were to return that evening, an entire chorus of those tiny frogs would serenade me. It would have been so easy to miss that little thing hopping near my foot. In fact, I might have stepped on him or her. I wish I'd heard them singing.

And the groundhog in my garden this past week. I stopped to watch what he would do. He did absolutely nothing because he sensed that he was being watched, but what if he *had* done something and I'd missed it?

Which brings me to a terrific baby I know. Every week, every time I see him, he is bigger, smarter, trying out new tricks. He laughs and laughs at his big brother's antics, which proves he has developed a sense of humor at twelve months old. It wasn't long ago that he was just sleeping and drinking. It would be easy to simply look at him and smile, but no, it's necessary to really have a good look at what he's doing this week that he wasn't doing last week if we are to understand the stages of life and how they work to make us who we are.

This brings me back to Montaigne and aging.

His recipe was down-to-earth. Now *he* lived with his eyes wide open, or so I believe.

According to Ms. Bakewell, his quest was to find solutions to things like this: Pay attention. Give up control. Be ordinary. Be imperfect. Guard your humanity.

What interests me about this is the difference between his thoughts and current thinking about how we should live:

perfectionism, the desire for power and control, the chasing of material goods, the quest for a bigger and better everything.

At the extreme opposite end of Montaigne's seemingly easygoing philosophy is the 2006 little book written by writer and filmmaker, the late Nora Ephron, on aging. It is called *I Feel Bad About My Neck: And Other Thoughts on Being a Woman.*

Ephron's dermatologist told her that our necks start to go at age 43. So if we want to think like Montaigne, we should form a club and remind one another that we don't care about our necks because we are bigger than they are, we are in charge of life, and necks do not count. I took myself to the dump with my bathroom scales not too long ago, as I got tired of being annoyed with myself for, as the French say, the matter of "*avoir du poids.*" As I drove off from that huge dumpster where my scales now lived, I waved bye-bye to them and said, "Go bother some other woman." Thus, I felt great relief. So salutary, so Montaigne of me.

Aging, although not in every circumstance, can be a cause for jubilation. So why do I think my age sounds better in French than it does in English, as the French rolls so elegantly off the tongue, with a smattering of *je ne sais quoi*? Montaigne, when referring to his own aging, declared that he tried to "increase it in weight," referring to its value. "The shorter my possession of life, the deeper and fuller I must make it."

When compared to the zeitgeist of current world affairs, it makes sense to greet each day with passion. The state of being happy is like an active verb at times. It takes diligence and a positive, seeking attitude.

Aging is often accompanied by widowhood. I'm not big on the word widow. It sounds a bit defeatist, harsh. The word widow reminds me of weeding, of clearing up the past, or winnowing. I say let the chaff blow where it will, but keep the good stuff, the grain, secreted away in that special compartment of my heart labelled Happy.

Dusk, Twilight, Dark
Winter Evenings or Summer Evenings?

I CANNOT DECIDE WHETHER I like winter evenings or summer evenings best. I don't know why I'd like to make up my mind about this small matter, but it has all got to do with light and how I long for it when it has gone, as on short winter evenings, yet pine for dark when I want comfort, as on long summer evenings.

Winter evenings offer something that summer evenings do not. Think about the cozy factor. Cozy is not a word that I would use to describe any summer evening that I can think of, unless we are talking about a campfire.

Hygge is the Danish word that is meant to bring contentment, along with the cozy factor writ large into our lives. The concept of *hygge* has been frequently introduced in North America so that chain stores that used to sell only books can pawn off blankets, mugs for hot drinks, soft throw cushions, and hot water bottles with fleecy coverings for the delight of our wintry evenings—as well as the overuse of our debit cards. And don't forget candles. Candles are the very hallmark of *hygge*. I suppose it's all to do with the soft light lulling you into a late dinner as the snow falls, softly, mind you, against the window. I notice that those who advertise the joys of *hygge* fail to advertise snow shovels along with their candles and throw cushions.

But there is admittedly a very attractive idea behind hygge. Who doesn't want comfort, warmth, a place to sit, cuddled into one's own blanket on a cold night? And you can't do that on a summer's eve.

But summer's eves offer long golden shadows from the old elms in my garden, more time to sit on the back porch with the glow of the little light bulbs my son strung up for me, more time to read and to listen to the birds' Choral Evensong as they settle for the night. So there is no arguing that longer daylight can be good for us.

But back to *hygge*. That can be good for us too. It's all a part of the balancing act of our lives.

Electricity, a book by Victoria Glendinning, which she wrote in 1995, is a finely tuned work of fiction that takes place during the ushering in of electricity into a country house in Victorian Britain. The heroine, Charlotte, lives at home with her parents and her widowed aunt, who dresses all in black. A dashing young man named Peter arrives to wire the electricity into the house. Charlotte falls in love with Peter and feels safe in the dark so that he cannot see her wrinkles, the flaws she perceives that have robbed her of her youthful beauty, and thus we understand that Charlotte has a lot to learn about life and what matters.

And on comes the light, and Peter proves himself a hero.

Once the room is lit up with electric power for the first time, the family questions whatever happened to those hours of half-light, "before the lamps were lit, those long, quiet passages between day and night?" It was their thinking time, when they used to sit and ponder the day, or read, or sew "while the earth turned."[1] And then followed the thrill of the oil lamps coming on gradually, lighting up the room. But now, all at once, it is ablaze with light, already leaving behind those softest of moments, now assigned to history.

So much for Charlotte and her wrinkles.

You do not want to know the end of this story, nor do I want to tell it. The thing is that since I read Ms. Glendinning's book in 1995, I have been waiting to talk about it, so you, my reading friends, are hearing about it now.

---

1. Glendinning, *Electricity*, 164

I like the word dusk. It's a softer word than dark, which I like to think of as being pitch dark. No point in half measures for these things. And there is also one of my favorite words to describe that time of day. Try this one: twilight. Twilight says it all. It reminds me of the winters of my childhood when we came in from school with frozen toes and put on our slippers, and in no time at all, we were all at the kitchen table with meatloaf and boiled potatoes and peas.

And now, in the summer twilight, I sit on my back porch with the little lightbulbs my son strung up for me and listen to the birdsong and read. As the weather cools, I wrap up in one of those *hygge* kind of blankets, the ones that can be found on the shelves that used to hold the non-fiction in the bookstore. Once swaddled, I search for something good to watch.

And then the dark and the fully lit lamps.

In that same fuller lighting, the corners of our homes and of our lives show us where the dust collects, where it sits waiting for us to sort it out, sweep it away, start afresh in the light of day.

"Lighten our darkness we beseech Thee, O Lord . . ."[2]

---

2. Anglican Church of Canada, *The Book of Common Prayer*, 63.

Marginalia

I CHERISH MY COPY of Hermione Lee's 762-page biography of Edith Wharton. Never have you seen pages so full of a reader's thoughts.

Some things are written in my best handwriting on the empty pages at the front. Others are underlined, and tiny reminders are noted in the margins of the appropriate page. Some are starred with emphasis, which in my personal marginalia language means "Never forget this!" And there are exclamation marks.

I know that this constitutes criminal activity according to many, to most, to all of my friends. But I can't help myself. It's one of the ways that I color my life. If I read something that hits hard, I never want to forget it, nor where I found it. I need to convince you to see my scribblings in a less harsh light.

Edith's Marriage to Teddy Wharton was not successful for a variety of reasons, according to both the book and to a man with whom I spoke who works in their historic home, 'The Mount,' in Lenox, Massachusetts.

Edith was part of the literati of the Gilded Age. Teddy was a sportsman and had no interest in literary pursuits. The marriage had been failing for some time, but Edith knew it was coming to an end when, on a train from New York City to Lenox, she told Teddy of her great interest in a book about heredity by Robert Lock. She had marked in the margins the things that she wanted to remember. (I knew I could count on you, Edith, for your marginalia.)

Teddy's response to her comments on the book was as short on understanding or caring as one could get. It left Edith flattened and aware that he was neither interested in her opinions nor her interests, nor, in fact, in her. She felt imprisoned. The fact that she was romantically involved with Morton Fullerton, combined with Teddy's alleged volatile temper, did nothing to move their personal story in the right direction.

Later, when Edith and Fullerton's affair was on a collision course, she spoke of her "Furies" and of how they danced in heavy boots in imitation of her own emotional condition.

The quote that I needed to capture most was this one from Bedier's retelling of Tristan and Iseult. "*Ni vous sans moi, ni moi sans vous.*"

My books are full of lively commentary. I hope that those who borrow them might enjoy my small, scribbled treasures. I hope too that if my children keep my books, they will consider my thoughts. Books speak to us in many ways; in the way in which the author intended, in the way in which the author did *not* intend, in the way the characters speak to us, in the way in which the reader interprets it, and in the comments to be found in the margins by other readers.

Edith grew up in a family with the surname of Jones in America's Gilded Age in New York City. The expression "keeping up with the Joneses" was a reference to her family. Her wealth did not shield her from heartache and disappointment. She carried on in her vain search for lasting joy.

She did care about her friends and offered one of them self-help by advising her to embellish her inner house so that in difficult times she could find comfort within herself.

This is my small salute to you, Edith, and to your tireless work for Belgian refugees post-World War One, for whom you built workshops and health care facilities in Paris.

Your life, your literary reputation, your travels appeared shiny and glamorous on the outside, even when the embers of your personal happiness had dimmed. You had some rebuilding to do,

Window Music

and you took your own advice. You brought light to hundreds of those who suffered great loss.
    You did what you could to decorate your own inner landscape.

Diane's Paintbox

FOR MANY YEARS, I have kept in my journal a beautiful postcard. It is full of bright ocean light off Mahone Bay in Nova Scotia. There is a yellow building with a red door and a patio. On that patio are trees, bright flowers, chairs, and a small table with a white umbrella for shade. I would like to sit there and have a cup of tea and a very long chat.

The sunlight falls all over that scene and bounces off that yellow building. There is a window ajar at the top. I have wondered who lived in it and thought about that fresh breeze right off the ocean going straight into the window. In fact, I'd like to live in that room. So not only would I like to have tea on the patio, but it seems that I want to take over the entire scene.

Many years ago, when I walked into my university residence for the first time, I met a girl named Diane. Diane Wile-Brumm and I have been friends since that day. It is Diane who painted this picture of the outdoor cafe among her many other sun-filled, salt-breeze-fueled paintings that show the viewer her love of life and nature. She paints sunflowers and tomatoes, domestic scenes, outlines of faces like Virginia Woolf's, with her lively colors. I could say much more, but Diane is modest.

Diane told me about the day she painted this particular piece on the postcard. She needed a break from the studio, went to the cafe for a cuppa, and sat in the ocean breeze thinking. I'm amazed that she ever got out of that chair. For me, that chair in that breeze in that scenery would spell "all day."

Friends are a bolt of light like nothing else. When we get to keep them as long as Diane and I have been friends, it's an even more brilliant light, just like the bold colors in Diane's paintbox.

Window Music

WITH THANKS TO THE late British writer, Ronald Blythe and his enchanting book, *Next to Nature: A Lifetime in the English Countryside*, I have discovered a creative thing to do early in the morning. It seems an enrichment towards the day ahead, and so far, my neighbors think so too.

Blythe declares that once upon a time, during the days of poet George Herbert, Christians had what was known as window music, which they sang out their open windows both mornings and evenings. I imagine that it was a way to greet the day and ask for blessing and sustenance. I wonder if it's true that poet Herbert both sang and played his lute out the morning window, even as he lay dying?

Window songs! In the morning! And in the evening! Maybe it was similar to Evensong. My curiosity was aroused. I searched everything I could for further information, but there was nothing to be found.

But I did get an idea. The dog walkers on this street and the university students are out early each morning in all seasons. I thought they deserved a bit of music to encourage them as they trod along, maybe still half asleep.

I am an early riser. Somebody has to do it, and it seemed a job tailored for me.

Advent One was the perfect place to begin. I cranked open my front room window a few inches, put my speaker on the sill

Window Music

and streamed the music for Handel's *Messiah*. I pumped it up a bit, just enough to lend some beauty to the chill of the morning.

A neighbor on whom I can count to come past at 9:00 every morning with her dog shouted in the window, "Lovely! Thank you!"

A few days later, I switched it up to Bach's "Christmas Oratorio." She stopped again, threw her arms up in the air and yelled, "It's celestial!"

Another dog, Sadie the Bernese Mountain dog, crossed the road when she heard the Handel but perked up her ears and came back to hear the Oratorio. *Requiescat in pace*, Sadie.

It was fun to see who cared and who didn't. No complaints, so I thought I'd carry on.

After Christmas, my window music became Mendelssohn's beauteous "Psalm 42, Opus 42." It was soft and soothing. I wasn't at the window at the right times to decide how it was affecting people, but I let it play for forty minutes and hoped it was a helpful way to begin a new day.

With Spring arrived the crash and bang of things unfurling like mad, so "Appalachian Spring" seemed the appropriate choice. Aaron Copland's music is so sensitive that you can feel the buds opening and imagine green things shooting up through the soil to begin again. The flute opens one flower, then another. Tenderness and new growth everywhere. Sometimes it is quiet, sometimes it is dynamic in imitation of the astonishing rebirth of the spring world.

This morning I found an old piece of music I thought worthy for my window music. The original was written by George Gershwin and was titled "Walking the Dog" from the 1937 musical *Shall We Dance?* I tried it out. I liked it, so I decided to try another song with the same title by the Rolling Stones. I liked that one even more. And if I were a dog-walker, I'd want to hear this song in the early morning, so that is next up. I'll be interested to see how the walkers respond, let alone their dogs.

Once the days get hot and hazy I'll try Gershwin's "Summertime."

It seems a positive way to refocus our thoughts and to light up the day ahead.

The Moon and Me

> "The moon was but a Chin of *Gold*
> A night or two *ago* —
> And now she turns her perfect *Face*
> Upon the world *below*—"
>
> EMILY DICKINSON

THERE IS A TINY village in southwest Scotland that has my heart.

In this village, there are a few streets lined with small cottages. Some have names like 'The Old Smithy,' or 'Rose Cottage.' All of them have windows, large ones that are smack on the narrow roadway. Whether you drive past or walk along the narrow siding, the lamplight in the windows beckons.

That comfortable hominess is what I love about the evening hours, as it throws its softening light on domesticity. Since there are no electric streetlamps in this place, these small scenes are wrapped round in a glow of their own making.

I find myself longing to belong there, on the inside, within the lamplight and the quietude of it, to be a part of the moment in that womb-like space.

In that cottage lives a poet. "What is he up to tonight?" I wonder. Trying to find words that rhyme with other words to carry along the flow of his thoughts? Writing a love letter to a woman far away? And what about the artist's house, she with her paint box spilling with scarlet, orange, pink, shades of blues, and pale yellow, the color of moonlight? What has she found to record in oils for tomorrow in the evening dim of her sitting room? And the church lady's house? Has she said her thankful prayers, put on her flannel nightgown?

The window in the village shop stays on all night to showcase the wares: chocolates and newspapers and cereal boxes and dish detergent, all lit up in an unearthly glow.

The coffee shop remains open even though it is past 10:00. The large stone fireplace throws warm light across the room. The pub in the basement, born in the 1500s, has neither caved to home reno shows nor modernization. It remains comfortable and still serves its ales to those who come for a chat.

Overhead, the moon, the biggest, brightest glow in the night sky, looks down on the quietened streets.

The moon and the sun are partners. They work together in perfect harmony. They've been doing the same thing since the beginning of time. Up, down, up, down. Your turn, my turn. One provides the light by day, the other the light by night. The perfect relationship. Day followed by the night.

That is the thing about contrasts. They come in pairs: large/small, happy/sad, warm/cold, slowly/quickly. They come in nouns, verbs, and adverbs. One without the other would be meaningless. Opposites are necessary to fully play out the scene, to lend understanding. Dark can be metaphorical, like evil itself or the feeling of walking into the unfathomable black of a strange room in an unfamiliar place. But we need the dark to tell us to stop working, to lull us into rest. Light feels friendly. We understand the world better in the light, recognize objects, know where it is safe to step.

After an evening in the village, it's a long drive up the hill to the old house in the wood. We sit upstairs as the light from the fireplace dances on the ceiling. We discuss the television news. Even the dog is content as he curls up at our feet.

And then to bed, down four steps and up another four to the familiar room, which I have come to think of as *mine* as opposed to the other friends who come and go.

Although it is time to close the huge wooden shutters on the bedroom window, I cannot do it. They will stay open all night as long as I am in residence.

They stay open because the moon is enormous, a deep orange orb hanging without strings to support it, up there of its own accord. She is looking in at me from the backdrop of total darkness. She has brought no stage crew to back up her performance every night. She is surrounded by stars that glisten and gleam. I do not see nighttime shows like this one in my highly electrified Canadian city.

Darkness. Light.

The scene, this much natural beauty, pinches a bit, hurts a little because I don't know what to do with it. I do not have enough words, a way to describe the beauty of that black sky with the splashes of purest gold. Nor is there a way to understand what goes on in the nighttime forest as the moon watches over the badgers and the deer beneath, and over the humans in this house as we crawl under the duvets and wish goodnight to the moon.

The Rach 3 Introduces the Sun

GOOD MORNING, MR. RACHMANINOFF!

I say *au revoir* to winter when I look out my east-facing front window.

Scarlet, underscored with orange, rips through the morning sky. Your Rach Three is making an entrance with the sunrise, a statement of the day ahead. The music unwraps tenderly, slowly, and before I know it, there is an explosion of sound along with the promise of new birth. It builds as the scarlet and orange screech, race further and further across the dawn cityscape until, at last, there she is: the sun.

In you, Ms. Sunshine, I see warmth, light and the promise that the cherry red branches of winter Dogwood will return to the lime green of Spring, that the small and graceful Amur Maple in my back garden will again unfurl into my own private green library as your leaves surround my porch and that the Kwanza tree will bloom with pink buds, a huge Happy Birthday balloon.

Children will careen down my small street on their scooters, race around the park, ask me to buy their lemonade.

And my small world will bask in your light.

The First Day of Spring

"Hope" is the thing with feathers—
That perches in the soul—"
Thank you, Emily Dickinson.

My first robin of the season this morning was singing on Sharon-next-door's roof as I was cracking my eggs. She watched me for a while (the robin did, not Sharon), and I wondered if she was drawn in by Gabriel Faure's *Cantique de Jean Racine* that was playing nearby to my open kitchen window.

It has been a few years since I've kept a proper journal. Six, in fact.

I have stacks of journals from yesteryear. I've been reading them again.

We had a life so rich and full, so rounded. If you don't catch the diurnal on paper or in poetry or painting or music, it slips away altogether like salmon swimming upstream in the spring run-off at Hidden Valley Park.

This evening, the quietude of Compline, thirty minutes of perfect peace in the pew, The Book of Common Prayer and music. I took it all in, knowing that this season's Shadow bursting into Light was designed to bring new life to the world, to me.

FRIDAY, MARCH 21ST, 2025

I have tulips, a rainbow of color in the ancient blue and white soup tureen on the dining table. Tulips are a splash of life when the well runs dry. Every time I walk past them, I think how lucky I am to see them there.

My sister, Jan, told me to put pennies in the water as the tulips benefit from the copper. It's not easy to find pennies since they've been discontinued, but I secreted some away, both for the tulips and for the ancient penny-loafers that linger in my closet, reminders of my youth.

TUESDAY, MARCH 25TH, 2025

I went for a walk at Bronte Harbour this morning. It's a forty-minute drive to that former little fishing village, then a right turn, and a left turn and there you have it, Lake Ontario in all its glory. And on a summer's day, there will be sailboats, the white sails flapping in the breeze.

The forty-minute drive means I can listen to my playlist all the way there and all the way back: Rod Stewart and his *Great American Songbook*, James Taylor and his "Shed A Little Light," Ella Fitzgerald, Leonard Cohen, Chris Botti, Creedence Clearwater Revival's "As Long as I Can See the Light," Mendelssohn's "Psalm 42, Opus 42," Erik Satie's "*Je Te Veux*," Albinoni's "Adagio in G Minor" and many others.

Walking along the harbor wall, I was bombarded with swallows. I don't know if they have returned to Capistrano, but they took up a lot of real estate in Bronte today. They darted and bounced overhead, and I do not believe they had a plan. They were simply having fun. Having fun is good.

I looked in the bird book when I got home. I noticed a tinge of blue on their wings, so I think they were tree swallows. I was lucky to see them.

THE FIRST DAY OF SPRING

WEDNESDAY, MARCH 26TH, 2025

A great chat with a dear friend at The Dundurn Market this afternoon. It doesn't take us long to get to the heart of any matter. And so we did.

I like that little coffee shop, which is a small market where they sell local produce, specialty teas, oats, homey things, and bunches of flowers. They have set aside three wooden tables for those who would like a quiet cup of something hot. I feel a bit as if I am in Paris while there, except for the Champs, the Eiffel Tower, the traffic, the streetscape, the language. In fact, it's nothing like Paris at all. Maybe it's just the small tables in the small space and the bit of funky that presides. Or maybe it's just me *wishing* that I was drinking hot tea with my good friend in The City of Light. But right here was perfect too.

Forgiven

I RECENTLY JOINED A discussion with a few friends concerning the Late Henri Nouwen's book *The Return of the Prodigal Son*.

In 1986, Henri Nouwen found himself in the unique position of being allowed to sit in front of Rembrandt's painting of the same subject for one entire week. It is held at The Hermitage in St. Petersburg, Russia.

It was a week that both fine-tuned Nouwen's understanding of the message within the story and deepened his relationship with God and with his earthly father as he presented the published book to him on his 90th birthday.

In the painting, we see the father so willing to receive the son whom he thought was lost forever. He has returned home after spending all his legacy from his father on the wrong things. In his sorrowful state and with broken spirit he asks his father for forgiveness. The father, in imitation of the Heavenly Father, holds his son in his arms and, immediately upon hearing his son beg for forgiveness, gives it wholeheartedly. There is no holding back, no scolding, no "Why did you?" but there is love and acceptance and most importantly, non-judgmental, immediate and total forgiveness.

At the right of the painting stands the older brother, the one who has stayed home, helped his father, has not been careless with either money or morality. What we notice most is his stern face, unflinching, staring at his kneeling, sorrowful younger brother locked in their father's arms. But it is that son, the older one, who cannot find it in himself to forgive either his younger brother for causing heartache over the years, or his father for not celebrating him as the good, careful son he himself has been.

The question arises, "Who else needs forgiveness?" Human pride can get in the way.

The background of the painting is dark, frightening because the viewer cannot see who or what is lurking there, but a beam of Heaven's light magnifies the father's embrace, the repentant's sorrowful condition and the sternness of the older son's facial features.

It is a reminder of the One who forgives without conditions. And it reminds me not to be the immovable force when it comes to forgiving others.

The Garden, the Sunshine, the Book

ONCE UPON A TIME, I took a book out to the garden. Our three children were young, but old enough to know that I was one minute away and right out the back door.

I had a lovely spot among the hollyhocks. I pulled up two lawn chairs, one for my feet and one for the rest of me. I arranged them in the right spot so that I could have my head in the shade and my legs in the sunshine.

I made it so that when I popped my head up from the book, I could see the perennials blooming all around me, the soft pink of the hollyhocks, the yellow of the Coreopsis, the deep blue spikes of the delphiniums.

I liked to think of myself as a bit like Cleopatra, floating along a glassy river on my barge, only my river was made of grass, and the lawn chairs were too rickety to float me anywhere.

While Cleopatra's subjects waited on her every whim, what I had to remember was that if I wanted a glass of ice water, I'd have to run into the kitchen to get it myself.

I put a pillow at my back to take the crick out of the lawn chair and another smaller pillow to take the crick out of my back.

"It's lovely," I thought to myself as I looked around my smallish Kingdom. The peonies were as rich, as splendid as possible.

So there I was, out there in my sublime small world, with my as-yet-unopened library book that was due in seven days. Iris Murdoch was never an easy read, but this one I was sure I could knock off if I kept at it.

I turned to page one. The neighbor shouted at me over the fence. I shouted back and we played a bit of verbal ping-pong before she noticed the book in my hand.

"I'll let you get at it," she called.

We had several dogs in those days (one at a time), and this one's name was Max. Brittany Spaniels are not known for their love of relaxation. I was on page five now. The book had captured my interest. By the time I got to page six, Max noticed that I was enjoying my reading. He appeared for a little pat and a bit of throw-the-ball-and-I'll-make-a-proper-nuisance-of-myself. And so we did.

I ignored the ringing phone indoors because who could possibly want me to get out of my comfort on a lovely day like this? It rang itself into quietude. I began page ten and looked up to contemplate who could have phoned me and let it ring that many times if it wasn't urgent. I went through my usual list of possibilities as to who might have landed in hospital, or who wanted me to do some baking for the church sale, or maybe it was my Chief Gardener saying he'd be home late due to heavy traffic or some work to finish. Or had someone called to offer me a Big Chance? What if I'd missed it? And what Big Chance could it possibly have been? And why would they offer it to *me*?

I was looking at the blooms on the coreopsis when I noticed a plastic bag sifting around in the light breeze. I got off the barge to catch it before it flew over the neighbor's fence. Nobody wants a plastic bag floating into their vegetable patch as if it's ready to snap up the carrots, the tomatoes, anything.

I reseated myself and repositioned the pillows. The dog was panting for a drink. I got up, rinsed out his bowl with the hose, gave him what he needed. I spent a moment telling him what a good boy he was and how honored I am to give him cold water when he was wearing a fur coat, and here I was out there in my flimsy cotton skirt.

I was up anyway, so I thought I'd take the ground beef out of the refrigerator to thaw a bit before dinner so our two oldest would be on time for their piano lessons.

Back outside and floating down the Nile, I promised myself that *nothing* would pull me out of it this time.

But the postman needed my signature on a package that I had ordered from a bookshop. Since I was only on page fourteen now in my current reading, I had no idea why I had ordered the one that just arrived.

But once I opened it (because I could not wait until later), the Barbara Pym novel I longed for fell out. Joy! I would read her *Excellent Women* some lovely afternoon in the garden.

Iris Murdoch and I got down to business. I turned to page fifteen and remembered how Iris could be a bit of a challenge at times.

I ploughed through the next few pages (page twenty-two now!), and the seductive warmth of a summer's afternoon carried me away.

Some fifteen minutes later, I jarred myself awake as a little person tried to pry my eyelids apart.

"Mommy? Are you in there?"

The youngest person in our household took my hand, and off we went indoors as his naptime was over. I tucked Iris Murdoch under my arm. I could read her another time, an afternoon when I would be alone. As life has it, there are, in my present life, years after this small story, many, many of those kinds of afternoons.

When I got inside, to the noise and the clatter, I wondered why I thought that being alone in our garden with the delphiniums was the panacea when all the sunshine I'd ever need was holding my hand and waiting for me right inside our house.

Back Porch, Special Glasses, the Eclipse

On April 8th, 2024, North Americans stood outdoors in every possible venue to see what was the first total eclipse visible in North America since 2017.

I joined the millions and sat on my back porch waiting. And waiting. I was terrified that my special glasses would fall down and I'd be blinded by the light, so I added a towel on my head that I could tuck into the top of my glasses. And I watched as a very orange sun (they say it wasn't orange at all, but that the eclipse glasses turned it orange) got eaten up bit by bit and bite by bite with the moon's deep, dark shadow. When the world went dark, the birds became frenetic, and the people in Churchill Park, a few blocks over, stopped cheering. All was silent. I was surrounded by something spectacular. I have heard that many people cried, although I did not, which is strange for a woman who can cry in a dog food advert.

Such a thrilling cosmic event. This universe. Who says it came about of its own accord?

A Little Window Music at Noon

In the book entitled *A Year of Wonder: Classical Music to Enjoy Day by Day*, the music for today is Frederick Delius' (1862–1934) "To be Sung of a Summer Night on the Water."

NEITHER IS IT NIGHT nor am I on the water, but I could not resist trying this new-to-me music at noon today.

I opened my window to the sunshine and onto the quiet street. Given that it is the Civic Holiday weekend, there were few people about. I think the goldfinches and the mourning doves enjoyed it. They haven't packed up and left town this weekend, as have the cottage owners and campers.

It is a charming piece, full of soprano voices singing to the sky, wordless, and full of soothing sound.

I can see why people might like to be on the water with this music. It kind of floats you along.

Floating along with no effort required on the part of the floatee is enticing indeed.

My Old Table, My Dining Room Chair, My Mug That Holds the Pens

(The above title comes to you with dreams of an updated writing space.)

SEEMS IT'S ALL ABOUT the writing room. At least that is what I've come to understand the more I read about writers and their surroundings.

Agatha Christie (1890–1976) remains one of my favorite storytellers. It is not her actual writing style that appeals to me, but her characters who populate the fictional village of St. Mary Mead (which, in the BBC presentation, is the real-life village of Nether Wallop in Hampshire), and other charming spots on the map. Her characters are the winning part as they tread carefully throughout the storyline of clues and missed clues to come finally to the denouement when all will be put to rest, sometimes literally. I have heard it said that Agatha wasn't fussy about her environs. She wished only for a reliable typewriter and a sturdy table. And look where *that* took her.

I have had occasion to be in the writing rooms of two writers I admire for their portrayal of life in the age in which they lived.

Edith Wharton (born 1862 in New York, died 1937 in France) had a most beautiful library room with a desk in her home in Lenox, Massachusetts. Her desk is far too lovely in my estimation to have anything that might involve coffee stains, ink spills, or her Pekinese dogs teething on the legs. What her alleged desk really deserves is good, high-quality polish and a vase of pink peonies on it so it can remain in the style to which it was accustomed. I can't imagine anyone getting down to business on a desk like that one, but according to folklore, the desk which I saw was a replica of the original. Nevertheless, she produced several good novels, all of which reflected the era in which she wrote them and, in particular, some replicas of people who had populated her early life.

Honore de Balzac lived in France from 1799 to 1850. His writing room was in the tiny, white cottage where he lived in Paris in the 16th arrondissement, in Passy. He had a large, sturdy writing desk which might have suited the needs of Ms. Christie, and a blood-red stained-glass window nearby, the light of which spilled all over his desk. I thought it represented the blood of the French Revolution very well and gave the desk extra charm. Although I recommend that you not follow my behavior in this instance, I did give his desk a light pat with my hand just so that I could touch base with his essence. I did it when the docent wasn't looking, which is a bit shameful when I think about it now. But otherwise, there was not much in there, although it was enough to hear that he often ran off through the back door and down the lane to fend off his creditors. I enjoy the thought of him wandering the streets of Paris in the black of night in his white nightgown and lighting up the darkness in his own fashion with a candle glowing in his candlestick.

I often read things about people's writing rooms and wonder why they need to be splendiferous. Writing is a labor of focus and concentration, and a need to have paper clips, a stapler, scraps of paper, extra pens in mugs and a place to put the tea if necessary. So why is it that I read about charming little rooms where papers are lined in neat precision and bookshelves close by so that the writer can spin on his or her ergonomic chair and reach without effort for exactly what he or she needs?

There will be no picture of my writing desk, mostly because there is no desk, but rather a second-hand wooden table we bought for the kids on which to do their homework when they were in high school. It is cramped near the sliding patio door, too far away to reach the bookshelves, a laptop that makes me cross, a mug full of highlighters and notes to myself, and a stack of relevant books jammed into the corner of the table near the printer.

    Writing is a hobby for me, not a profession. It gives me joy and makes me think about life. That is not to say that I might need to jazz it up a little in my cramped space.

    But regardless of the no-nonsense table on which I depend to hold up the stuff around me, the words spill out anyway.

    The thing is, you see, I sit beside that huge glass window sliding door I mentioned with another window in front of me.

    The light streams in and helps the process along, no end.

Mrs. Fithian

Upon looking at a portrait in The Smithsonian American Art Museum in Washington, DC, titled We Both Must Fade (Mrs. Fithian).

THERE IS NOTHING LEFT behind of you now, save the portrait.

Lily Martin Spencer painted you in oils in 1869 as you stood before her easel in your blue satin gown, lace panels of purest white caught up around you, draping over unblemished shoulders, pearls clasped at your bosom and entwined through slender fingers, an aristocratic rosary of sorts. Toes clad in white satin slippers peek out from beneath the hemline that forms a hopeful ocean of blue.

Where were you going, Mrs. Fithian? For what distant land did you set your sails?

I stopped to stare at you. I wondered how you spent your days in real time, not when you were posing for Miss Lily Martin Spencer.

It was my immediate impression that you were not the Captain of your own ship, Mrs. Fithian, if you will excuse the comparison with the blue waves of your fulsome gown.

MRS. FITHIAN

Were you useful, Mrs. Fithian? Did you have a name other than your married honorific? Were you Elizabeth, Emily, or Jane? Augusta or Miriam?

Down through the years, you hang there, idly, in the Smithsonian, causing no trouble, minding your manners as you've been taught, content to float around in your blue skirts, known only as Mrs. Fithian, which gives your viewers no clues as to what went on inside your head.

But for a minute, if I may, I must get back to those tiny, square-toed white shoes you are wearing. Can you walk in them? Do they pinch and hurt, but come in handy for portraits?

Were you no one other than Mrs. Fithian, even to yourself? Or was it a case of existing like the woman in *Of Mice And Men*, the character known only as Curly's wife, who remained nameless, insignificant? Did Mr. Fithian refer to you as Dear, or Darling, or not at all?

What exactly did you do, Mrs. Fithian, when you weren't wearing a satin gown? Did you know how to peel spuds, change a baby's bottom, get your hands dirty, hang out clothes to snap in the breeze?

Were you a dab hand at growing roses like the one I planted in our garden, the variety known as the 'Wife of Bath' from *Canterbury Tales*, Chaucer's character who lived with renewed zest in spite of losing her outward youth and beauty?

I don't see it that way. By looking at your coy expression, I would say that you, Mrs. Fithian, were obedient, not used to calling your own shots.

Perhaps your purpose was to be lovely for Mr. Fithian, was it? Was it Mr. Fithian who wanted you to be cast eternally in your doe-eyed, powdered, crimped countenance? To live in a near-miss of a Victorian Bell Jar? His trophy?

I wonder what Fithian would have said had you got those lily-white hands deep in the muck of his horse barns? Did you join him on the hunt, race laughing on horseback over the green fields, the wind blowing your hair in all directions? Or did you stay home to await his plunder from the skies? Pluck the blood-soaked feathers? Stuff the grouse with bread, onion, sage? Pop them into the oven? Or was that job of other women, those who were employed to do the kitchen work to spare you and to uphold Mr. Fithian's reputation?

What would Mr. Fithian have said if you had announced your interest in a course of study in Higher Learning? If you had announced interest in something that had nothing to do with excellence at needlework or the pianoforte? Something cerebral, that allowed you to breathe fresh air?

And speaking of breathing, Mrs. Fithian, did you remain all strapped up under that gown of yours in a slimming contraption like my grandmother used to wear, a huge carapace of flesh-colored satin undergirded with elastic and whalebone so that when she hung it on the bedroom chair every night it looked like a part of the dinosaur display at The Royal Ontario Museum? No woman whom I have ever seen has a waistline like yours, pinched and stifled like a Royal Doulton Lady's.

It is the pale pink rose and the title of the painting that amuses me. "We both shall fade," it says. Of course, you, me, all of us will. If you approve of the Victorian notion of beauty fading as you age then go for it by all means or tell Lily Martin Spencer to think up another title for her work, maybe something like "The Older I Get the Smarter I Am," or "I Might Be Fading on the Outside but What's Going on in the Inside Has Never Looked Back."

If you could do it all again, Mrs. Fithian, would you do it differently? Would you slip off the stays, undo the corset, exchange the satin slippers for sturdy walking shoes, hike in the countryside? Enjoy the wind in your face? Let it mess up your hair? Would you let a little oxygen in?

There is hope! I can see what the artist has done at the window. The heavy damask draperies are pulled back. Sunlight streams in, lights up your face, the lilywhite flesh of your shoulders, your arms. You have a tiny grin.

Are you thinking what I'm thinking that you're thinking?

"It's time to hoist up the main sail!"

Today

I opened the door this morning while night was fading into day.

The sky was misty in the distance with a tint of pink. I could hear the traffic's roar along the highway.

Better yet, there was a massed choir of birds singing from the treetops.

A new day is born, with all of its possibilities.

I sat in the sunshine on the patio at the coffee shop on the lake for two hours this afternoon with a good friend. Sunshine changes the point of view. Even the boats so soon back in their docks looked happy. The sparrows were flapping around us, hoping we'd share some crumbs.

And this evening, a walk in the park. The willow trees have opened!

Maybe, surrounded in the arms of the Dundas valley, the air is warmer and more nurturing so that the greening of the world begins earlier than it does where I live just a few miles over.

THURSDAY, APRIL 24, 2025

The painter is here to do the bathroom and the little hallway across from it. He has removed all the mirrors. I'm used to seeing myself in the bathroom mirror when I'm brushing my teeth, drying my hair.

Window Music

Out of habit, I pop my head up from the sink, and there I am. But I'm not there at the moment. I'm greeted by a blank wall with grey putty on it.

Without the light's reflection, I cannot locate myself.

Outside Spaces and Inside Places

LIGHT COMES TO US in its own distinct manner.

For Group of Seven painter Lawren Harris, it broke over the mountains and shone on Maligne Lake in his 1924 painting of the same name. Chilean poet and diplomat Pablo Neruda wrote in his "Ode to Enchanted Light" about how the light makes a green tracery of interwoven branches, like latticework.

In my own small outside space is the tree that I have nurtured since it was only a shoot that persisted, popping up out of the trunk after its parent had been chopped down. Ten years later, I have a huge Amur Maple, considered a pest tree by many, as it replants itself and pops up anywhere, like in a childlike game of 'Hide and Go Seek.' I think it is a beautiful tree. It provides dark, cooling shade in extreme heat, privacy when I want to read out there, and it is green, green, green. When I need it most, the sun breaks through the top of the crown to remind me that it's still up there, up there in the sky and not to be forgotten. It is the sun breaking through that keeps the orange Million Bells and the ferns in the planters on the railings thriving, and the big blue bowl full of yellow and hot pink flowers flowing over the side of the pot. My outside space pleases me. It is nature's doing, not mine. I only water the plants when they look thirsty and deadhead them to let new growth spring up. The natural world thrives in that small space, including the groundhog who has shown up recently and might even be living under the porch.

Window Music

Friends in a nearby city once had a beautiful, tiny eating place in their garden. They referred to it as 'Provence.' Jill would say, "Can you come for lunch in Provence next week?" and of course we would. There was a table and four chairs with a vine-covered pergola overhead, a view of the steeples below the hill, colorful and artistic decorations hanging from the small tree lit up by the sun, a garden of delights in a row on the edge of the hill. Jill served salad in pottery bowls with strips of Parmesan right off the block, colorful summer food and fruit. And there was caramel ice cream. It was light and friendship rolled into one.

Inside light is of two varieties: what I call real light and fake light. In my small house, the real light pours in the front window every morning once the sun begins its ascent, splashes its palette all over the sky and waves goodbye as it heads off west. I give it twenty minutes, and once it has bled its colors up there, it is so bright that I have to pull the blinds back down to preserve the titles of the books on the shelves that get bleached in its glow.

And there is what I call fake light, the light that electricity brings us. I love lamps, not only for their light, especially the light they provide on dark winter evenings, but for their beauty. I don't have lamps that aren't beautiful, save one. And that one belonged to my in-laws. It is a floor lamp. It has a shade that was white and is now gray, a stand that was once straight and is now crooked. You pull it on and off with an ancient chain. I fear it might tip over someday. It stood beside my father-in-law's armchair. I like thinking about him pulling that chain on Sunday evenings to brighten up the room so they could turn on the television and watch Lawrence Welk.

I have a favorite lamp. We found it in Eastern Ontario in an antique shop called '1812.' It was a vase once upon a time until someone gave it a chance at a second life. It is soft blue and white porcelain, which somebody wired, stuck a light bulb on top, added a satin shade, *et voila*, a lamp! It sits on the kitchen table and lights up my breakfast, my lunch, my dinner.

At Christmastime, I bought eight little fake dollar-store candles that you switch on from the bottom. And I put them on the dinner table in small glass containers. It was safer than candles around my granddaughters and their long hair, and as calming as can be.

Inside. Outside.

The necessity and comfort of light.

Bright and Beautiful

> "All things bright and beautiful,
> All creatures great and small..."
> CECIL FRANCES ALEXANDER

ROGER TORY PETERSON, IN his *Field Guide to the Birds: Eastern Land and Water Birds*, tells me that the beautiful bird that sang his way to my back porch this morning was a Baltimore Oriole. He was dressed in feathers of the brightest orange. It was an early morning thrill for me and a fortunate way to begin this new May day. I stopped everything and held my breath in case he heard me.

I am told that they breed in elm trees, including in Ontario, which makes me feel better about the huge overbearing elms that reach up from my back garden as far as Jupiter, the same ones that I am afraid could come down in a storm. This new information bestows them with a bit of extra panache.

Their song is a low whistle. I heard it from where I was sitting in the back room. The other little bird, a sparrow, dashed away the minute he heard it.

And on Ken-next-door's fence, what I see morning, noon, and evening is a bright, golden trifecta of goldfinches. They have their own kind of fun as they bob around for the sunflower seeds in the feeder. They scoot if something larger lands on the fence, looking for a share of the treasure too. They are beautiful creatures. I wonder what they will do if the oriole checks into their space? They might fly off as they do when other birds arrive. Timid, I guess.

Here, right here, is where my life unfolds, right on this tiny piece of creation. It reminds me of how much I take for granted.

At the end of her beautiful book, *The Backyard Bird Chronicles*, writer Amy Tan mentions that she has a special bird in her life, one who watches her in fact, and after he has had a good look to see what she's up to, he goes back to his own affairs.

I've yet to find a bird who watches me, but I'll keep looking for one that might. In the meantime, I'll continue to enjoy looking at their antics. It must be so much fun to fly.

Into the Light

First Peter, verse 9, reminds us that we have been called out of darkness and into the light; light that is marvelous in fact.

What a welcome thought that is.

Every time of year has its special features. If we took a vote on it, many hands would go up in favor of spring.

I love that spring unfolds at Easter when we have two kinds of Resurrections to celebrate. First, the lifesaving one, the main event that enabled Jesus to rise again and create Heaven for mankind.

Spring also brings other kinds of joys, ones that are lesser than the Easter story but demonstrate it and are redolent with their own specific beauty as reminders of new life and starting over.

I noticed this past week that the forsythia seems a deeper shade of yellow this year, and the magnolia buds outside the house down the street are a deeper pink than I have seen before. The hellebores in the park have spread, have more maroon blooms nodding in the breeze. The willow trees are dripping down to the grass and are greener than green, or does it seem that way because I missed all of this beauty during the ice-laden days of winter?

Nothing can thrive without light, neither trees, nor daffodils, nor ducklings, nor the vegetables that nurture us, nor children, nor you, nor me.

When we walk in the light that we are invited into, the shadows fall behind us. The requirement is that we recognize the marvelous in it and will share it, will spread it and nurture it like a gardener enriching the soil.

Grace is the key to amending that particular kind of soil.

The Literary Salon and How to Have One

A LITERARY SALON IS all about exploring the riches of one's heart.

Contrary to what I had believed, it seems that *les grandes dames Parisiennes* were not the first to start that noble tradition during the sixteenth and seventeenth centuries. Others got there first. The poet and scholar, Al-Khanas, recited her poetry *en plein air* in Mecca as far back as the pre-Islamic period. Thus began literary salons for Arabic women.

One hundred years ago, Chinese women in a remote part of Hunan province started their own salons, although the word salon was never applied to what they did to share their knowledge.

Because girls were forbidden an education, the women developed their own writing system, *nüshu*, which translates literally from the Chinese as "women's writing." It was an orderly system based on characters in long columns in right-to-left order. *Nüshu* was embraced and closely held as a tender secret. It was meant for women only. It provided a way in which they could share their poetry, hold private conversations, tell of their sorrows and speak of their joys. The idea, I'm convinced, is worthy of the designation *salon*.

The romance of the salon took root for me in my early days during a seventeenth-century French literature course. The learning style, the friendships that emerged during the salons, the discovery of new ideas appealed to me.

It resurfaced when I had three tiny children. The time to hold the salon was not going to be *then*. I let the notion ripen for all those years until recently.

A few summers led us down to Massachusetts, to Lenox, where we stopped at the former home of Edith Wharton. It was a refreshing place to visit with its Italianate garden overlooking Laurel Lake. We sat on Edith's sweep of a veranda under the big blue sky, and I channeled my inner *Saloniste*. Edith once said that it takes the same modicum of care to plan a proper salon as it does a soufflé. She often hosted salons when she lived in Paris.

A few summers ago, a friend had her book of poetry published. Our late friend Janine and I agreed that Margaret's flowing, meaningful poems needed to be shared with others.

I told her about my heart's desire, and we did what all smart girls do. We planned a salon.

Janine lived in the countryside amidst a big shady patch of green. Her garden spilled over with wildflowers that brightened up a summer's eve like little pops of fireworks. Every summer, she erected a huge tent and filled it with chairs, electric lamps (outdoors!), carpets and tables. I called it 'Little Bloomsbury' with reference to Virginia Woolf, Vanessa Bell, Duncan Grant, and the others. Our original plan was to hold the salon outdoors, but a dripping curtain of July rain put a stop to that. Enter Plan B: we moved indoors.

Margaret's poems are lit up from within. Her words floated through the warm July evening. Music sifted in and out of her syllables as the cello strung her words together like a fine necklace of pearls. We were creating a seamless weave of poetry and music.

Then dinner. Rain was dashing down with that calming, drumming sound that only summer rain can make. The windows were open wide. A long table awaited us, laden with vases of pink, white, and mauve hydrangeas, jars of wildflowers, pottery bowls of salad, bread, cheese, scoops of ice cream from the local creamery for "afters." There was green tea in tiny crockery cups, and all of this splendor lay upon a huge piece of India print cloth.

Our host read aloud to us over tea an article by C.S. Lewis. It was followed by a satisfying discussion.

All that is needed for this grand recipe is as follows: a few friends, twilight, simple food, some pickings from your garden, a sprinkle of music, enough worthy readings to maintain interest and generate discussion. Sitting around the fireplace in winter would work as do deck chairs on the porch or inside in summer. Eight friends are enough to keep the conversation moving.

Early French salons were often held in the salonniere's boudoir. As she reclined in bed, her friends gathered around on chairs to listen to her hold forth. While that is not the style these days, I'd be happy to repeat the way it worked on that perfect summer's eve.

The thrumming of summer rain brings out all kinds of emotions in me, but this was special.

The Intersection of Light and Love

CONTRAST IS EVERYTHING IN art, poetry, music, and nature. It is contrast that takes a painting or a piece of music from flat to fulsome. Imagine, for example, *The Goldberg Variations* without that lovely, soft, sleepy bit at the beginning, the "I'm just waking up" moments before the tempo changes to frenetic.

In the painting under discussion, the subject, a young girl, is twelve years old. Her wan figure lies in the stark white shroud-like sheeting. Her arm lies flat at her side, reaching out, possibly in a gesture for help, or perhaps merely in need of the warm reassurance of a familiar hand. Her dark hair falls across the pillow. The fly that sits on her arm is an ominous sign, a forecast perhaps. Something in the dark shadow behind her resting place alarms the viewer. What is this painting trying to tell us? What is happening to this beautiful child?

In the Musée Des Beaux Arts de Montréal hangs this oil on canvas painted by Gabriel Max in 1878. It is entitled *The Raising of Jairus' Daughter*. It was first displayed in that same year at the Exposition in Paris.

The story of Jairus' Daughter can be found in the Books of Matthew, Mark, and Luke, the Synoptic Gospels, so called because they all relate the story in the same way. Therein lies the story of one man's plea to Jesus as his little daughter lay dying. He begged Jesus to lay his hands on her and heal her.

This story, this painting, coalesced something in me. I could not saunter past, couldn't walk away. I stopped and sat for a while. The guard told me that it has the same effect on many people. It speaks to them as it was speaking to me.

The artist had imbued a certain softness in the profile of Jesus, in his cheekbone, in his lowered right eye as he looked upon the sleeping child, and in the manner in which he held her small white hand in his, thumb tenderly folded into her palm, his fingers wrapped around hers. Comfort there. Love.

But there is hope. At Jesus' side lay soft pink roses, a small bouquet, a promise of renewal. The child is enfolded in Light.

The words in Matthew, Chapter 5, verse 42 tell the rest of the story, the story of hope and healing, of faith and fulfillment.

"... In the foul rag and bone shop of my heart."
—William Butler Yeats (1865–1939)

I've promised myself that I will think about one new thing every day. It seems a good thing to be doing.

That small quote has always interested me, and I have just now read the whole poem, "The Circus Animals' Desertion," by Irish poet William Butler Yeats, from which it is derived. It was published in his *Last Poems* in 1939.

I have assumed that small quote was about past pain and past joys that he has bundled into a title of eight neat, concise words and tucked into his memory bank.

I could do with further instruction than that which I have already read by the critics, but in the meantime, I'll settle for a simple explanation in the way in which I have interpreted it. Isn't that what art is for? To see it for what it holds for ourselves?

I see it as his reference to the dusty corners of our lives, the things we stow away to either forget or to recall in old age. We protect these sad or happy events in the Do Not Discard pile.

Like the rag and bone man's shed, where he deposits the ephemera he collects, memories collect dust, too. The human heart is the shop where we store the past in whatever form it takes. Happy. Sad. Opposites depend upon one another to distinguish them. Balance is all.

When we need a bit of light, we can unearth the motherlode.

A World of Light

My friend Edith lent me her favorite book when she heard me say that I wanted to write essays about light. She handed me a 1976 copy of the late American poet May Sarton's *A World of Light*, the pages yellowed and falling, the whole of it wrapped with care in a small plastic bag, a rubber band holding it together. That kind of care speaks to loving a book.

In this book, May Sarton has chosen several friends who lit up her life in one way or another. The one with whom I am acquainted is Elizabeth Bowen, the Anglo-Irish writer about whom I have read in the diaries of former Canadian diplomat Charles Ritchie. I have enjoyed reading many of Bowen's own books.

May Sarton describes a time in London in her youth (although she doesn't mention the year) when the world opened up to her in the unexpected ways that youth often brings. She was renting a room in a house in London, England, and met the fellow rooming beside her, who played the harpsichord. Bach's music filtered through his wall into her own space. May was interested in art, in music, in writing, in everything that London had to offer.

The harpsichordist asked her if she would like to come to dinner with him at his friend Elizabeth Bowen's house.

Ms. Sarton admitted to both terror and excitement at the prospect of dinner with Ms. Bowen, as she was well aware of her literary reputation.

She dressed in her blue evening coat and they took a cab to the beautiful Nash Terrace, that lane of superb white joined-up homes that faces Regent's Park. She stood shaking with fear at the pillars of the front door.

She described the sitting room with its French windows open onto the street scene, and the leafy glade of the June night alight by streetlamps. Leaves. Light. A June evening. If you're about to have dinner with a famous writer, it sounds like a worthy combination.[1]

She was excited by the company of Isaiah Berlin, Elizabeth Bowen's husband David Cameron, and David Cecil, whose biography of Cowper she had read.

She admits to being dazzled like a moth in the evening light.

On the mantel sat a bowl of white peonies that were reflected in the mirror above it. There was laughter all around her, and she felt a jab of culture shock as she stood paralyzed, trying to sort out the nuances of Oxford English.

In spite of the sad fact that their long friendship came to an end, May Sarton never forgot her evening in all of that splendid London drama and light.

---

1. Sarton, *A World of Light*, 192.

A Little Window Music, Continued

THIS MORNING'S WINDOW MUSIC experiment was fun. I tried out the 'Walking the Dog' music but decided that the Gershwin original was more suitable than the Rolling Stones version. And then it streamed into some of his other music, which was fine too.

It seems that my dog-walking public loves me. Two of them said how happy it makes them on a beautiful morning to hear music on the street. They laughed and laughed when I told them the name of the tune, as they had a dog on a leash with them. So I invited them in. And as it happens, I discovered deep roots to my own past in one of the women.

It was an early morning 'one off' fueled by light and laughter.

And by a sweet dog who slept on the carpet and looked as if he'd have been content to stay for the day.

En Route

I HAVE FINISHED READING Alison Light's memoir, *A Radical Romance*, of her marriage to Raphael Samuel, British Marxist and Communist Party member. In her memoir, she dealt with the grief of losing him, not in a maudlin way, but in a literary way. Her style in doing so felt safer to read than maudlin. Writing made her less afraid, she declared.

She posits that for our friends who have passed on, we can compare our grief to a valuable thread that is woven into our lives, but for the partner whom we have lost, it feels more like the entirety of the tapestry.

Her memoir has left me thinking that the challenge is to find an alternate way to think about loss. Those glorious threads that we wove in and out and spun together into an entire carpet of meaning for years, can they not be made useful in other ways? We get to carry the best of those we love with us forever, but sometimes memories are not enough.

Although what we had can be taken from us in the physical sense, it can never be taken in the metaphysical sense. There is a plan beyond our human frailties, and although it doesn't stop the missing and the continuation of the love, it is the Light at the end of the tunnel that one must grasp hold of. And in the meantime, all the conditions of humankind can do with our help and our attention.

Without that knowledge, I fear that I, we, all of us would be lost. Our tapestries are not meant to have been woven in vain.

Fellows of the Royal Society

DURING THE PANDEMIC, THE Royal Society of Literature in England invited people to write short entries using the taped interviews from their extensive library. The idea was that this series, *Only Connect*, would help to do just that, in a world that had suddenly gone quiet. I chose interviews with people whose lives I thought spoke in some way about light and how they had introduced it into their days.

I have permission from The Royal Society to reuse these short pieces here for my purposes.

MICHAEL PALIN

Michael Palin became a Fellow of the Royal Society of Literature in its 200th year. My reasons for choosing his interview will be made clear below. He has been writing all his life, including diaries, notebooks, plays, scripts and novels. He was known to me for his comic roles in Monty Python's Flying Circus.

I clicked on his interview video and kept at it as I liked hearing him say, "It's much easier to be nice to people," as opposed to getting angry. That seemed a refreshing thing to hear at this time on planet Earth.

When I was in my early twenties and a single working woman in Ontario, I looked forward to watching Monty Python on Friday evenings, beaming out of WNED in Buffalo, New York.

My co-workers did the same. On Monday mornings back at the office, we compared notes. The Python's 'Ministry of Silly Walks' was the big hit in the government ministry in which I worked, with the 'Dead Parrot' episode close on its heels.

On and on it went. This tale says a lot about the Python's status. They were a special commodity and not to be missed.

The most salient portion of this interview, however, for me, concerned Palin's worldwide travels during the filming of *Around the World in 80 Days*.

His initial concern was figuring out his actual role within the documentary, but the fact that he could be himself came about in a lovely way.

The crew needed a dhow or boat to get them from Oman to their filming location. Indian fishermen came to their rescue. Neither spoke the other's language. It mattered not. They figured out one another's intent and had a time of warm-hearted friendship. Palin was moved by the experience. He commented that often in the West, people are judged by what they have, not by what is inside. We forget to separate actors from their roles. His comment was so un-Pythonesque that it took me by surprise. It seems a suitable thing to be thinking about during this time period in our history.

P.D. JAMES

The P.D. James interview was conducted by Peter Kemp, Val McDermid, Mark Lawson and Melvyn Bragg.

'P.D. James A Celebration' is a heartfelt discussion by her writerly friends who talk about her world and her person with love and admiration. She excelled at researching the grizzly bits and then wrote about how hate can twist the human heart into evil. But it was her stalwart positivity that impressed the panelists.

She had a sad childhood, which she hid from her writing. Some suggest that her Inspector Dalgliesh was herself incognito. Perhaps. But what set her apart was her insistence on a strong moral path that led her readers away from the evils committed in her writing. She was a stalwart Anglican, a defender of the wisdom folded into *The Book of Common Prayer* and of all things that pointed towards a higher enlightenment. Her motto was akin to "We can get through this. We will be fine."

The ending of her books leads the reader from darkness into light, often with mention of nature as "the last wisp of white smoke drifted over the sea." Even Dalgliesh falls in love at the end of *The Murder Room*. We have the satisfaction of knowing that he will be happy now.

Baroness James was able to draw hope out of hardship. We need her endings that point to the natural world resuming its course. We need to read about that "white tumble of clouds" at the end of her book *The Lighthouse*.

Her positivity and her unwavering faith are salutary.

Sunday-ness

FOR THOSE INTERESTED IN the life and work of Canadian artist Emily Carr, the book to read is *Corresponding Influence: Selected Letters of Emily Carr and Ira Dilworth*, edited by Linda M. Morra, University of Toronto Press, 2006.

Ira Dilworth (1894–1962) was her closest and dearest friend. He was the British Columbia Regional Director of CBC Radio.

Dilworth had a Sunday evening broadcast known as Sanctuary. Emily looked forward every Sunday evening to Ira's program of soft poetry, music, all of it chosen for its calm and peace.

In her letter to Dilworth after hearing his program on January 18, 1942, she thanked him for his programming, for what Emily referred to as the "Sunday-ness" feeling behind it, and for the fact that it helped her to settle for the night.

Her concept of Sunday-ness has changed in Canada. It was common in the forties, fifties, and sixties for families to attend synagogue services on Saturday or church on Sunday. That habit became ingrained and a vital part of family culture, which often included not only lessons of a religious nature but also the inclusion of grandparents for dinner and quiet family time together.

For Emily, Sunday-ness meant attendance with her family as a child and into her adult life at the Church of Our Lord in Victoria, BC. The church stands there now, in Carpenter Gothic style, charming, welcoming, historic. The books she wrote mention it so often that we know it took a special place in her philosophy.

Window Music

At Christmas of 1941, Emily wrote to Dilworth thanking him for playing a recording of her "work hymn" among the carols. It meant something special to her.

Emily was referring to the hymn she sang each time she began a new painting and each time she dipped her brush into her oil paints. I like to imagine her standing in the deep, heavy old-growth forest, thanking the Creator for the world around her and asking for help in replicating it.

Her work hymn she refers to was "Breathe on Me Breath of God." There are four verses. The one that makes me think of her is verse three. It was written by Rev. Edwin Hatch in 1878.

> "Breathe on me, Breath of God,
> Till I am wholly Thine,
> Until this earthly part of me
> Glows with Thy fire divine."

Emily depended on the forest and on her beloved friends in the West Coast communities to accept her in the same way in which she embraced them. The Ucluelet people on Vancouver Island christened her Klee Wyck, which translates to Laughing One. She lived among them in her tiny caravan with her pet monkey, Woo.

In recent years, she has come under criticism for her paintings of West Coast peoples as a non-member of that group. It seems the most unfair accusation. As it happens, one of her paintings shouts out loud about the pain that she felt both for nature and for the future of humanity. She would be saddened to know that after all these years since her 1945 death, she would be criticized for her innocent, passionate response to nature and to her paintings of the culture of her Indigenous friends, whom she loved.

One of her greatest concerns was the deforestation by the lumber barons and their desire to clear-cut the forests to produce lumber and, therefore, wealth.

In particular, one of her paintings moves both the emotions and, in my opinion, her reputation forward. Emily painted it in 1935. It is a tall rectangular canvas that highlights the huge, forever sky behind it and one spindly tree that has been stripped in hopes that it would be perfect to be cut down, logged and sent away for money. Instead, it has been found wanting by the lumber barons. It has not made the grade and will not be useful for profit. It has lost its purpose. There is something inherently human in this portrait of a tree. It stands denuded, embarrassed, and ashamed as we all would be if solitary and judged with nobody to defend us. It proclaims loneliness and singleness. The trees around it have all been found worthy. The chosen ones have been carted off, but not this one. It stands undefended as the imperfect one.

But there is redemption in this painting. There is hope. Carr has titled it *Scorned as Timber, Beloved of the Sky*.

There are times when we all feel abandoned and alone. But behind that tree is a stream of Light that beams down on it, enfolds it, supports its hopelessness, makes it whole.

We may feel scorned at times, but we are never scorned by him who breathed life into us.

Even when we fail to measure up, we are worthy.

This is a bit of Sunday-ness for you, Emily. With my gratitude.

A Little More Window Music

THIS MILD SUNDAY MORNING seemed a good time to open up the front window and share some music with my neighbors. For those who don't recognize what I call my "Sunday music," it wouldn't be offensive, and for those who do, they might enjoy hearing it, all of the tunes among the classical Church of England repertoire. I am careful not to offend the sensibilities of others, as respecting one another's beliefs is a key to civilized society.

The Cambridge Singers supplied this small road with a stream of beautiful music this morning: "To Thine Be The Glory," "All Creatures of Our God and King," "Love Divine All Loves Excelling," "My Song Is Love Unknown," "King of Glory," and others.

For me, this is the music that exemplifies the Light that generated the world.

Flowers

"The world is charged with the grandeur of God"
GERARD MANLEY HOPKINS

AT THE BEGINNING OF the book, *Mrs. Delany: Her Life and Her Flowers*, British Museum Press, 1980, the late Ruth Hayden included a warm oil painting titled *Portrait of Mrs. Delany* by John Opie, National Portrait Gallery, London.

Mary Delany was born in 1700 in Coulston, a village in Wiltshire. Her family was in service to the Crown, which provided her with experiences that other children were not able to access. As a small example, her aunt and uncle were in charge of her education and arranged for Handel to play Mary's own harpsichord for her.

In the head and shoulder's frontispiece portrait of Mrs. Delany, she wears a black shawl over a white dress, and around her neck a locket, allegedly a gift from Queen Charlotte, strung around with seed pearls in the shape of a heart, which is topped with a red ribbon of what might be rubies. Around her head and face, she wears a white lace ruffle, which is perhaps an attempt to play up her kind appearance, her rosy complexion, the steady, brown-eyed gaze, the intelligence of her face. The white ruffle is topped by a black mantilla.

Window Music

As it happened, King George III and Queen Charlotte were devotees of Mrs. Delany and made her friend, the diarist Fanny Burney, Keeper of the Robes for Queen Charlotte.

All of this background is meant to point towards one of those instances that some put down to coincidence, but I am convinced that there is more planned ahead for us than is mere chance. When new people walk into my life, I recognize them as a part of a skein of connectivity that has been spun for me, that kind of connectivity that is available to all of us. The challenge is to either pick it up or leave it where we find it.

In 2003, I attended a gathering of writers in London, England, who used the New Cavendish Club for overnight stays. When I went down to the breakfast room the next morning, there seated at a table for two was a beautiful, silver-haired woman who asked, "Would you care to join me for breakfast?" and I replied, "I would."

Her name was Ruth Hayden.

Was this good fortune, happenstance, preplanning, or "*beshert*" as an elderly friend used to declare when she thought things were working out by decree from the Divine? It's either that or thinking that life is just one big crash and bang of coincidence. Friendships, both old and new, are another way that light manifests itself. Just when you need a jolt, that light bulb that sits waiting in your brain switches on, and there it is. And sometimes these meetings lead to new knowledge and another chain of events.

Ruth told me about the book she had written about Mrs. Delany and about how Mrs. Delany, at age seventy-two, decided to do something about her love of paper cutting art. Ruth suggested that I go to the archives in the British Museum and stop in the museum bookshop to find a copy of her book. I did buy a copy, and it sits beside me now as I type this. I was welcomed into the archives and was handed a pair of white gloves and a huge box. I opened it and spent a wonderful couple of hours holding the paperwork artistry that Mary Delany created so long ago with her steady hands and a pair of scissors after her hours of researching botanics.

Backed by backgrounds of black paper, I held in my hands her brilliant red poppy, the stamens and pistils, the seed pods, the hanging yet unopened blossoms ready to pop, the leaves, one of them so expertly cut that it appears to have turned in on itself. There is *Rosa spinosissima*, the Burnet Rose, along with well-executed sixty-five tiny thorns, and on the page opposite it *Rosa x damascena*, a perfect and realistic insect bite cut out of a leaf.

Enter Canadian writer Molly Peacock in 2015 with her new book, *The Paper Garden: Mrs. Delany Begins Her Life's Work at 72*, McClelland & Stewart. I spied that book sitting on a shelf at my local bookshop and took it immediately to the desk. I knew I had uncovered yet another treasure and would need to digest every word of it. I loved the mentions of Ruth Hayden, whom the author had interviewed at length, and of her own labors concerning the same subject and of how Mrs. Delany loved placing her artistic flowers against black backgrounds.

What was I to do next? I needed to complete the story, so I dropped an email to Molly Peacock through her publisher explaining my delight at finding her book. And then a note back from Molly agreeing with me about Ruth's grace and *joie de vie*.

And then, years later, in 2023, a birthday card from a dear friend with a note on it saying that she had found this lovely card with floral artwork done by a Mrs. Delany, who began her life's work at 72 and retired at 88 in 1788. I've tucked the card into the book along with the letters from Ruth.

My meeting with Ruth was like obeying a sign that said "Go" as I walked straight ahead into the unbridled pleasure of a huge new piece of learning, over eggs and toast.

Had I ignored Ruth's invitation to breakfast, none of this would have happened, and I would not have the lovely memories, nor the two books on my shelves, nor my birthday card with Mrs. Delany's paper art of *rubus odoratus* on the front, nor the letters from Ruth that continued our friendship via the old-fashioned post.

This is my salute to both Mary Delany and Ruth Hayden, both of whom did not let aging put them off their game. They pointed the way, with fresh ideas in their heads, one for her visual art, the other for her literary art.

Life is better with each other in it.

The More, the Merrier

"In addition to ordinary teas there are numerous varieties flavored with dried flower blossoms. Most popular are chrysanthemum, jasmine, lotus, hibiscus and rose. The dried flowers are generally left in the tea to expand beautifully and aromatically during infusion."

—Routhier, Nicole, *Foods of Vietnam*, Stewart, Tabori & Chang, New York, 1989.

Combine all of those beautiful flower blossoms in the quote above into one happy teapot, and you'd have the perfect solution for a better world.

The cookbook from which I have extracted the quote was a gift to me several years ago from my dear friend Nguyen Phuong Thao. Thao and her late, wonderful husband Dr. Do Trong and their three children sit at the beginning of a long tale, a story of mixing flavors, of learning, loving, sharing, tasting, laughing, crying, succeeding; a story of how the life of my late husband and of my life and the lives of our three children were changed from the inside out. A story of possibilities, of what can happen when we allow a world of flavors into our teapots.

As South Vietnam fell to Communist rule, small fishing boats packed with grandmothers, babies, teenagers, parents, toddlers, crept away, often under a darkened, starless night, into the perils of the South China Sea.

With fortune, their journeys ended in one of the several camps that had been set up by the United Nations High Commission for Refugees. The camps were ready for the thousands of people who would eventually make their way to their shores with the hopes that one of the Western countries would accept them. Canadians rose to the occasion with aplomb and with welcome committees all over this country.

The Federal Government at that time asked Canadians to set up community groups of friends, churches, professional groups, neighborhoods, any group that could register as a charity through the Government of Canada and organize themselves to raise funds to sponsor and provide initial care for a person or a family.

In Hamilton, Ontario, the Mountain Fund to Help the Boat People was born. In quick order, the Fund had registered with the government, had opened a bank account, had advertised for help through cable television, and had acquired the use of a rental property that was offered as a settlement house by friends of the founder.

Over the next several years, those flowers in the teapot got a glorious workout as they blended and brewed. Men, women, children, too many to count, arrived regularly at Toronto airport carrying with them what they had, often nothing more than official papers from UNHCR, their legitimate proof of a new chance of belonging.

During a twelve-year period, the Mountain Fund members watched a multitude of newcomers arrive. Their successes challenged the human spirit to soar, to conquer, to become much-needed pieces to complete the story in the jigsaw of the great Canadian landscape.

That is only the beginning of the story of how flavors blossom and mix, offer up new tales to be told, new panaceas for heartache, new generations to tell their ancestors' stories down throughout the future.

Window Music

Years later, we added new friendships from Iran, from Syria, to this exciting human mix. Some of it came about because of a longtime friend whom we had met years before due to our joint interest in what was happening in the South China Sea. And here she was, years later, introducing me to new Syrian friends. That is how life works if we let it. It is like a huge spider's web of connections, beautifully and carefully woven and too precious to wipe away without considering the geometry that went into it.

Our teapot has new flavors added in, like the brilliant red pomegranate seeds, which are mixed into the Syrian *kibbeh*.

Recently, Nigeria has arrived with a great helping of fun into the circle, and Afghanistan too is playing a blessed role, and yes, I'd love to come back to enjoy more of your *Kabuli Palaw*.

Life is what we make it. Just as we blend spices and blossoms and seasoning into our cooking, our lives deserve the same flavors. It does not happen by locking ourselves into groups of our own traditions. Peace comes with looking into the eyes of others, by seeing one another's pain and by sharing our joys. We must invite it in and consider ourselves blessed when the invitation to friendship is returned.

On my refrigerator door is a typed Vietnamese message that translates to "The more, the merrier."

What a glorious party it is when we all sit down at the same dinner table.

Summertime

THIS MORNING'S WINDOW MUSIC was George Gershwin's "Summertime." I played it in order to imitate the current heat wave. It streamed into a million beautiful pieces, but one I had not heard before took top prize. It is called "The Armed Man: A Mass for Peace," by Karl Jenkins. It is appropriate for this time in the world; beautiful, played by the London Philharmonic. I didn't have time to peek out the window to see what was happening in the street with dogs and their owners, although I did notice one woman zipping along. She was dogless, as am I, but I did see her glance this way. I wonder what she was thinking. Maybe it was "I wish that window music woman would move to another location." It is possible she might have been thinking that. She did have a bit of a scowl. We don't all like the same things in this life. Or perhaps she was thinking, and rightly so, "I wish that woman would focus less on the music and more on getting rid of her weeds."

The flowers and ferns on the back porch are in full glory but in need of lots of water to survive this heat wave.

The Princess Diana clematis is blossoming. I look forward to it every summer, and this year it is crawling all over the porch railing. Its tulip-shaped, deep pink cups sit upwards, rather than facing down. It is one splendid flowering vine.

Friends came to visit this afternoon. I wanted us to be outside under my lime green umbrella on the porch, but it was too hot, so we stayed inside and drank tea, eating biscuits and cheese, talking

Window Music

about Barbara Pym's novels and summer plans and the current world order, most of which does not get our approval.

    I am thankful for good friends. Friends are a huge light source in our days. I can say that mine are all smart and very funny.

    I hope they love seeing me as much as I love seeing them.

Surge, Illuminare

"Rise, shine"

Isaiah 60:1

When we look at the round, silken faces of newborns, we wonder what those sweet little people will do with their lives. How to help form them into good people? How to inspire them to be themselves, not what others think they should be? How to help them become exemplars of sowing light?

Here follows an abridged true story of a little girl who grew up to use light in a way that would affect social change in the most dramatic of ways.

On May 24th, 1870, in Malmesbury, England, Mr. Alfred Seeley, manager of the Silk Works, and his wife Caroline presented the world with a baby girl, never knowing for one minute that their little Alice would change the politics of a country a continent away.

I like to imagine Alice's birthdate as a day when the River Avon sparkled in the sunlight, the jackdaws cawed on the abbey rooftop, the daffodils streamed down the bank to meet the river.

As little Alice stretched and mewed in her cot, nobody yet knew that far-flung corners of the earth awaited her arrival many years later.

Window Music

It was this same Alice who eventually became Lady Alice Seeley Harris. Her marriage to Revd. John Harris and their trip to Congo as missionaries with the Regions Beyond mission (1898–1906) had everything to do with the events that would change King Leopold of Belgium's hold on the Congo and on the vile rubber trade inside of it.

Someone gave Alice a Kodak camera before she left for Congo. It is surmised that the gift was from Dr. Harry Guinness, the head of the mission, but that is unproven, as others still assert that it was not a Kodak but was a German-made camera. I don't want to argue with Mark Twain, who subsequently wrote King Leopold's Soliloquy, where he talked about the Kodak camera being the one witness that he could not bribe.

Into the mission station, Alice marched, and into the hearts of the Congolese people who needed the outside world to hear of the unspeakable abuses they suffered at the hands of the Belgian rubber traders.

And in Alice's capable hands was the camera that took the glass slides that proved her shocking stories of limbs that had been cut off children and adults alike by the Belgian overseers as punishment for not working hard enough, for not collecting their daily rubber quota. Due to her photographic images, she and John were funded to take their magic lantern show throughout England and into Europe and America to speak to anyone who would listen to them. The Congo Reform Movement grew alongside it. Audiences wept. Political voices grew louder as Alice spoke with John Harris's occasional slap on the stage floor of the rhino-hide chicotte that the Belgians used to whip the natives. That the world be rid of the Belgian King was top of mind. King Leopold's greed had been exposed, his cruelty revealed. Alice's lantern slides were shown in parish halls and theatres, on any stage where John and Alice could speak to the public and raise awareness of the tragedy that was Congo.

Years later, T. Jack Thompson, former director of The Centre for the Study of Christianity in the Non-Western World at the University of Edinburgh, declared in his book *Light On Darkness*, that he believed Alice Harris to be the missionary whose photography carried the most import in the Congo Reform campaign.

How did these magic lantern shows work? The magic lantern had a concave mirror behind a light source, which in turn directed light through a small piece of glass. These were called lantern slides.

So it was all due to the light.

There are many forms of light and many ways of incorporating it into our lives. Alice had her way, and it changed everything. The king was removed, and the Belgian government took over the administration until 1960.

Had Alice's parents, on the day of her birth, had any idea of the challenges their daughter had ahead of her, it would have been cause for their great worry. But Alice did as was required. She went about her work energized by the *Light of the World*.

Alice rose. And she shone.

All of the women mentioned in this small book have done their fair share of shining.

Canada Day
True Patriot Love

THIS MORNING, A FULL sun. I awoke with thanksgiving for my birthright.

I had no idea of my good fortune until I was in my thirties and began to meet people who had switched places in the world, not by choice, but due to bad politics that produced wars.

Having my birthright means that our children and grandchildren also are the beneficiaries of this blessed freedom. Ever cautious we must remain. Democracy can slip right through your fingers faster than you can say "We stand on guard for thee."

I've often wondered what is expected of us on Canada Day other than fireworks and BBQs.

I decided this morning that I'd best make something of it in the way of celebration. I took myself to the newly renovated coffee shop on the corner. There was a jazz band playing in the entrance, the floors were new, and the counters had been switched out to faux marble. The bulky furniture was gone, and the windows were more obvious to make the space airier and lighter. I sat on the patio with my Skinny Chai Latte. It was sunny with a breeze, and I sat there for the best part of two hours.

There is something about sitting alone in a public place that demands some sort of different action, and I wondered why I hadn't brought a book to read or my phone to play with and scroll through so I would look as busy as everyone else who was fiddling around with their phones. And then I remembered that for 90%

of my life I did not own a phone and made out well without one. And nor did I need a book. "Whatever happened," I asked myself, "to sitting and taking in the street ballet?" as Jane Jacobs referred to the passing scenery. So that is what I did. I noticed the walkers, the dogs, the babies in pushcarts, the summer students who have arrived at the university. And I eavesdropped on the conversation at the next table over, not on purpose but because there was nobody else on that small patio but myself and the next table over. They were talking loudly, and I heard it and was sorry that it wasn't more up my alley, but I unwittingly learned a great deal about water conservation.

And of course, I was thinking about my new friend Montaigne and how he would have encouraged this in me, this way of living by the carpe diem method and making the best of the situation. I had, in fact, switched the *on* button to living in the moment.

I could be the decision maker, could stay until I no longer wanted to. It was all mine to choose. I was emboldened. I was the coffee-shop boss of me. Had I brought along my phone or a book, I would have been purposely dismissing my surroundings. I'd not have had the fullness of the situation, that simplistic Montaigne moment of embracing life as it unfolds. It is enough to sit alone and take in the sunshine, the breeze and the scenery.

And then, because things generally work out, I find, along came two good friends who sat at my table and we chatted for forty minutes about the state of things and about our mutual love of country.

It was the perfect way to celebrate Canada Day, and I didn't even have to plan anything.

But I'm questioning a few things today. I'm wondering if we should replace the statues that were splattered with paint and torn down, considering that they are a part of our history, the story of Canada, of how we got here. We need to view history's mistakes as a chance to get it better, and at the same time, we need to take pride in why we have the right to exist as a sovereign nation. We weaken ourselves when we say, "We didn't like our history, so we tore it down, threw it out, cancelled it." It points to us not being grown-ups, not being capable of claiming and learning from our past and taking hold of our future. We have much to celebrate. Strong countries are not afraid of looking backwards in a grown-up way.

Canada does its grand share of respecting those who come to escape hardship and seek us as a second chance. There is nothing like an airport hug that says "Welcome!" That is when the light streams down on both the helper and the helpee. Never should we overlook the fact that both sides of the equation are helped.

And because we claim to respect life, why have we cancelled the sanctity in both birth and death, the pair of which are a part of the drivers in the human experience and both of which have value beyond mere human understanding? Reclaiming that fact can only help us regain our respect for all conditions of humankind.

No fireworks and BBQs can preserve that.

Happy 158th Birthday, Canada!

A Little More Window Music

AT 9:19 A.M.

THE SUN IS BRIGHT and there has been a little rain overnight. It will help those once colorful, now sere and falling-to-bits plants on the porch that I am trying to keep alive.

The window music this morning is Mendelssohn's "Psalm 95." I thought it appropriate, as the current study I am attending focuses on the Psalms.

It is beautiful music with which to eat breakfast.

LATER, SAME DAY:

Last year, I read a riveting book by Jared Brock called *The Road to Dawn: Josiah Henson and the Story that Sparked the Civil War*. It involves the evolution of the Underground Railroad for escaped slaves from the US. I have been leafing through it again this afternoon and thinking about the remarkable nature of how Henson and his family got to Canada.

In short, Josiah Henson was an escaped slave. He hid his wife and children in the woods while he walked miles to find help. He noticed a schooner in the water nearby. He met a series of men en route who introduced him to a Scottish captain named Burnham, who owned that boat. He asked the captain how far Canada was.

The captain caught on immediately and asked him if he was running away.

Josiah replied in the affirmative, knowing that his family was hidden in the woods and wondering if the man would report him to the slave hunters.

The captain told Josiah to go and get them.

Captain Burnham was able to get them on a boat headed to Canada, and the rest is history.

Whenever I read that, it strikes me how easy it is to say, "Go and get your family and get on my boat."

Get on my boat.

So easy.

"Get on" is driven by a Light bigger than ourselves.

A Light full of Grace.

The Dam Seed Catalogue

"If you have a garden and a library, you have everything you need."
MARCUS TULLIUS CICERO

"HAS THE DAM SEED Catalogue arrived yet?" We began every December by asking one another that question.

The Dam Seed Company is one of Southern Ontario's treasures. It relaxes out there on Highway 8 amongst rolling grass and pristine white buildings as it waits for us to do our annual Spring shopping. It arrived just one day after the Winter Solstice, and we leafed through the pages planning our next garden.

At least I was doing the leafing, and The Mister was doing the speaking part, where he said, "But we don't have any room for more plants."

And just in case I didn't hear it the first time, he repeated it with feeling, "But we don't have room!"

We kept an uncomplicated footprint and planted a bold and beautiful streamer of zinnias every spring in the back garden. The mildew-resistant zinnia seeds blasted into blooms in brilliant ribbons of color. They danced among the cosmos and the nasturtiums all summer long until late September. It was our own tiny jewel box of a garden with thanks to Mother Nature.

Window Music

Henry James was the one who proclaimed that summer afternoons are the two most beautiful words in the English language. On those August days when the elongated golden rays weave in and out of shade, our zinnias popped like fireworks in the back garden.

They needed nothing to set them afire; in their own right, they were light, and color, and movement. The hummingbirds embraced them. Swallowtail butterflies and monarch (yes!) butterflies sifted among them in their own version of The Royal Lepidoptera Ballet.

Sometimes the red, yellow, and hot pink zinnias propped themselves up in a clay jug on our pine table in happy bunches. On occasion, we set them in vases against the soft blonde wood of the altar table at church. The pages of the latest catalogue offered a litany of florals that sang of Spring and rich soil.

Two entire pages dedicated themselves to celebrating pollinators. The decline of insects is a global issue. Had we bought some borage seed, it said, we would have blue flowers that would bloom even in cold weather so that the bees might have a banqueting table even after other blooms withered.

Borage! I fell smack in the middle of a Barbara Pym novel on seeing that word in print. I decided we needed some borage seeds. I mentioned it.

"But we have no more room!"

It's right there on the list of pollinators: basil, borage, buddleja...

And then I spy the list that starts with P: parsley, presicaria, phacelia, poppy...

Those words help me to remember what Spring feels like when we hear the clear whistle of the returning Baltimore Orioles and see the rich green of the cardinal vine leaves and the lime of the moss around the old tree trunk.

I spotted a hybrid of hollyhock I'd not heard of before: Halo Mix # 2628!

How did we miss this little beauty? "Brightly bi-coloured flowers that sparkle in the cottage garden," the description read.

And there I was again, safe in the bosom of childhood as my sister and I turned the blooms upside down to make dancing ladies in their ball gowns. They whirled and twirled to our imagined music and floated in their pink and maroon silk.

Larkspur, lavender, lavateria, lupins. My heart still jumps at the word lupins. I've always wanted lupins.

Oh, the glories held in those little white envelopes at Dam Seeds in the numbered bins! The miracle of it when I think of how dull, how plain are the thin, pathetic-looking little brown zinnia seeds in the bottom of the envelopes.

The tomatoes eventually wiggled their way up the vines, and with any fortune, we nabbed them before the raccoons did. Their nectar ran down our chins as we bit into them, whole.

"Nasturtiums: the catalogue continued. "Dwarf Jewel Double Mixed." We bought them every year and threaded the seeds with the zinnias. They bloomed into a border of happy just along the top of the soil, a carpet for the zinnias to tap-dance.

Our garden was not special in the world of gardens. It was not a rival to Sissinghurst like the cultured and famous one created by Vita Sackville-West. There were no garden tours, no newspaper articles extolling its beauty. The beauty was ours.

We all do our best with what we've been given. Bit by bit. That's how it works.

"Four o'clocks and foxgloves, snapdragons, stocks, and sweet peas . . ."

The Light in the Story of the Picture in the Frame

A CARDBOARD TUBE ARRIVED at my home several years ago, compliments of the recently deceased Richard Harris, grandson of Sir John Hobbis Harris and Lady Alice Seeley Harris. Inside the tube was a copy of a pencil sketch by British artist, the late Mick Bensley, formerly of Rottingdean, East Suffolk, England. He specialized in landscape and marine rescue art.

I have this month had the contents of the cardboard tube framed. It is easy to see why Richard Harris chose Mr. Bensley to sketch the scene on the Congo River, given the artist's love of the sea and water.

In another essay in this collection, I have talked about the true Congo story regarding the rubber trade and the Harris's input with bringing down King Leopold of Belgium's heavy-handed, cruel reign on the Congolese population. John and Alice Harris were in Congo as missionaries from 1898–1906. They had no idea what they were walking into, but they stayed and fought for the Congolese population until the end.

John Harris had called for a European Commission of Enquiry with regard to the cruelty to the rubber workers by the Belgian overseers.

In my newly framed picture, we see a steamship in a resting place on the Congo River, the smokestack belching into the sky.

Rubber trees in the background are eerie, plenteous, prophetic. They would play a key role in the testimonies that the Judges had come to hear. The rubber trees on the riverbank would serve to remind the panel from Europe how the latex that flowed through their veins had made the King of Belgium wealthy while at the same time introducing the Congolese people to the Belgian overseers' inhumanity. Although it cannot be seen in this picture, the name Archiduchesse Stephanie was painted on the boat's siding. It was her father, King Leopold II of Belgium, who was renowned for bringing the rubber trade crimes to the Congo. His appointed overseers were responsible for killing and torturing millions of Congolese who were punished for not getting their daily quota of rubber sap. Leopold's endgame was to become wealthy on the backs of the rubber workers. His plan worked.

On the Congo River in the picture, we see seven canoes, each carrying from seven to five men in white togas, standing and using poles to dig through the heavy waters to greet the boat and to meet, finally, the members of The Commission of Inquiry into Leopold's crimes against humanity.

On board were the three European judges appointed by Leopold himself in his belief that they would defend him. He was in for a surprise. The men were Dr. Edward Jansens from Belgium, Baron Nisco from Italy, and Monsieur DeSchumacher from Switzerland.

On the boat sat the judges, the Harrises, the European visitors. The canoes came closer. The Congolese people were invited to come on deck to tell their horrific stories.

Chief Lontulu, who did not speak English, nor did the Judges speak Lingala, laid a large blood-red cloth on the deck of the ship. He placed a twig on the cloth for each man, woman and child in his tiny village who had lost their lives to the Belgian overseers. There were one hundred and fifty twigs on the cloth.

Each story was worse than the previous one. The judges whom Leopold had appointed were overwhelmed, one of them to tears.

The decision was an easy one. Leopold was to hand over the administration of the Congo to the Belgian government. His days as King of the Congo were over. Thus, the rubber trade ended, but it was not until June 30th, 1960, that the Congo was released from Belgian control and taken over by France for a short period. In August 1960, it became the Republic of Congo.

It was Alice Harris's camera and her glass lantern slides that had initiated this quest in Europe. They knew that the stories they had listened to from the Congolese people were true. They had met the men, women, and children who had suffered unspeakable abuses for not fulfilling their rubber quota.

Alice's lantern slides, those tiny five-inch by five-inch glass slides that I held in my gloved hands at Anti-Slavery International Headquarters in Brixton, London, tell the truth. The evidence is real. The pictures do not lie.

This is a tragic story in a book of essays that is meant to shed light, to give us hope. And although it was too late for so many, the idea of light brought release from the worst of inhumanity.

Alice knew that the same light of love that she had trusted all of her life was speaking through her pictures. It was through the light in her lantern projector that made it possible for those in Europe and America to see the truth.

My sketch of the Congo River jury has been framed with a wide white border, then a slim maroon border inside that one and a strip of gold colored border against the picture itself. The maroon border represents Chief Lontulu and the cloth he laid on the deck floor to tell his story. The gold border represents the light that Alice's photos brought to the fore.

I salute you, Alice. You were a brave woman at the tail end of the Victorian era, when most young women were at home paying homage to what other people required of them. You left your security to illuminate evil and to bring relief and political change to people, strangers to you, across an ocean.

You rose. You shone.

Utter, Lovely, Chaos

This was the summer week of my family getting together, the most cherished thing I can think of.

Those recently tiny, adorable kids have grown into their preteens, leaving behind their adoration of grandma for their adoration of each other, of the latest music, of the most recent linguistic expressions. I have discovered that if I were what they refer to as being "riz" I'd be dandy. Riz, as I was told by my son, is now a short form of the adjective charismatic, meaning full of life and worthy of adoration, which is the reason they don't label me as being riz, but recent songwriters and singers have, it seems, made the grade. And nobody ever wants to be called a "Karen," which is code for some kind of cranky, bossy woman. They speak in a new kind of way that leaves me in the dust. "What on earth are they talking about?" I ask myself.

Sometimes I outsmart them, like when I told them not to go down to the horrible one-hundred-year-old basement, which I see as dust-producing, and they see as a kind of private clubhouse. What they don't know is that when they do go down there, the adults in the living room can hear every word they say as the furnace vent leads straight down to their conversations. I can't wait until they read this.

This was a week full of empty glasses on the kitchen counter, and I had no idea I owned so many. There were plates with crumbs and pizza crusts on them, chips on the sofa and bowls with wooden sticks in them, which indicated that someone had enjoyed the frozen ice cream treats I'd put in the freezer compartment for them. There were two pre-teen girls huddled in concert in the back room with the door closed, *sotte voce* whenever I walked in, and an almost twelve-year-old boy with a different soccer team shirt every day, playing soccer games on my iPad. The ten-year-old darling played rough and tumble with her aunt and otherwise had her own amusements in her favorite chair. And there was a new chihuahua added into the mix who managed his affairs very well in spite of the ear-splitting noise.

And since we couldn't all get our acts together to be here at the same night for a family member's birthday party we had two birthday parties, one on Wednesday night and one on Friday night, and I did note that when everyone had left there was a higher count of empty glasses on the counter top and again I asked myself, "since when did I own so many glasses?"

And in between times a surprise visit from old friends from far away, friends who are family to us, friends who shared our children's early years, which produced an onset of hugging and a flow of non-stop conversation.

And just because the kids discovered the wonderful things in this little area where I live inside of this big city there was pressure, subtle at first and then slowly building until it filled up more space, to visit the Korean Corn Dog take-out for Chun Chung, the Bubble Tea shop and the store that sells trinkets which is what I think of as junk shop for cheap merchandise but they see as akin to something like Tiffany's.

One of the uncles decided that he should take the kids to those mild amusements while the rest of us sat back and ate more pizza until they all got back with their trinkets, laughing at something that must have happened en route but with nobody spilling the secret.

At the end of Birthday Party #2, they all hugged goodbye on the sidewalk and got into their cars and drove off as I waved from the porch. I tried to be a big girl, but they are my family, and now they had left. My heart felt emptied out.

I was happy in the end about the dishes, the empty pizza boxes, the remainder of the birthday cake and the general chaos in the back room. I've just reminded myself that this past week should not be labeled chaos. The light that carried the week, I've decided, does not have a relationship with chaos. If I understand the bare bones of chaos theory properly, it is about deconstructing or a state of disorder, not constructing in the way that we had relived both loving family ties and old friendships.

I'm changing the title of this essay to Utter, Lovely, Order.

The Dwindling of the Light

IN THE BOOK *YEAR of Wonder*, by Clemency Burton-Hill, there is an introduction to a piece of classical music each day for a full year.

The book was a birthday gift. It is a treasure.

This morning's Window Music came from Thomas Tallis, 1505–1585.

He is called "the undisputed greatest English composer of his generation" by the author. His impact on Reformation English church music was profound. Tallis was peripatetic to say the least. With each change of monarch, his music adapted. With Henry VIII, it was Latin Catholic music, and following the break with Rome (1532–1533), the music switched to Latin Anglican music. When nine-year-old Edward took over the throne, the services had to be sung in English. Tallis worked hard to please every monarch's predilection. He has left us with a rich complement of wonderful sound.

This morning, I played his "If ye love me," softly out of my Sunday morning window, sung by the Cambridge Singers and led by John Rutter.

Clemency Burton-Hill says that Tallis left behind "some of the greatest treasures of the entire canon."

My own favorite from the Service of Compline is "*Te lucis ante terminum*," which refers to the dwindling of the light.

"Before the ending of the day,

THE DWINDLING OF THE LIGHT

Creator of the world, we pray
That with thy wonted favour thou
Wouldst be our Guard and Keeper now."

The Front Lawn, the Neighbors, the Little Library

MY BROTHER-IN-LAW COULD HAVE been the world's best architect. Move over Le Corbusier. He drew up some fine plans as to how a little lawn library should look. His drawings are in precise, neat pencil, measured, exact. They look like something you might want to frame. And that's just the drawings. He drew up plans for two shelves, both of them high enough to hold all books great and small. He left one side open, top to bottom, to accommodate extra-tall books.

One sunny day, they arrived after a three-hour drive to get here and hauled out of the back of the car the box part of the library and the sturdy pole to nail it to. Off he went to buy cement mix so that when he dug a hole in the ground, he could fix it into the front lawn. He and my sister had painted it turquoise with a lime green door around the plexiglass and a pink doorknob in memory of our mom, who loved pink sheets, pink towels, pink upholstery, pink flowers, and pink cushions.

Before long it was standing firm on the lawn waiting for customers, a book bastion which no man could destroy.

It was certainly an upgrade of the pretend library my sister and I ran out of our bedroom when we were small. Books lined the rim of the bed so that our pretend customers could see if they would rather read *Uncle Wiggly*, *Anne of Green Gables*, *Little*

Women, *Toby Tyler Joins the Circus*, *Robinson Crusoe*, *Black Beauty*, *The Wind in the Willows*, or *Nancy Drew*. We took turns being librarians and pretended to smoke crayons as we'd stamp little bits of paper with scribbled renewal dates. The little library on my front lawn has brought a certain measure of happiness to this tiny street and to myself along with it.

People come on bikes, on scooters, in baby strollers, on skateboards and on their legs. They stop to check out the contents.

I've met many nice dogs and many of their owners who stop. There have been visits from poodles, spaniels, mongrels, a dachshund, black labs, and chihuahuas. I often remember to put some dog bones in the library so the dogs can have a treat too. I asked one faithful fellow who drops by often with his spaniel, "What is your dog's name?"

"I hate to tell you," he replied.

"Is it Judy?" I asked.

"Yes. I'm afraid it is."

One woman rode her bike for miles from downtown across the waterfront trail to get to the library. "You've got the best books," she told me. "I come here because there are always mysteries." And so, to whoever leaves the mysteries in there, I thank you.

Someone leaves copies of the *Scientific American* magazine, which pleases another neighbor no end. Last week, I noticed a stack of children's books, so I assume that a mother somewhere in the environs spent quality time cleaning out her children's closets. There are lots of romance novels which find themselves permanent homes early, as well as classic novels and others who aren't quite in the classical canon, like those of Elizabeth Bowen, or old copies of the plays of David Hare. I recognize what people have studied at the nearby university when I check out the contents. Someone around here was an English major.

And they use it for other things, as did the person who put in little foil twists of succulent plants for other neighbors to take home to plant, and the beautiful bookmarks from a neighbor's worthy stamp collection, which she arranged and laminated. At

Halloween, there are spooky pencils from the dollar store for little fingers to take home. And often dog biscuits.

At times, I leave small notes taped to the window to point out special books that I know a particular person would like. At other times, I tape literary quotes to the window. The point of this essay is to tell you how much fun it is to watch neighbors enjoying this book box and coming together to say "Hi! What are you reading?"

Light walks down the street to see what's in that library. As one fellow said with glee, "And there are no late fees!"

I can claim limited credit for its success, as my own bookshelves inside the house are weighed down with things that I think I might like to read again but should share with my neighbors.

I have fun chatting with you.

Keep coming.

You'll recognize it by the pink doorknob.

Nighttime Windows

I'VE ALREADY DECLARED MYSELF to you in terms of how I love looking into other people's nighttime windows.

But there is more.

You need to understand that it doesn't involve me standing on a ladder with binoculars in hand.

I'm not so nosy as all that. It's the quick view I'm after, that which belongs to the casual passerby.

I'm after the comfort of the domestic, which belongs to writers like Marcel Proust in *Swann's Way* with his ladders of light reflected on the bed covering, or Vita Sackville-West in her 1931 novel *All Passion Spent* with the way in which she described Lady Slane's "pink shaded lamps and Turkey rug."

I extend this peculiarity of mine, in which I am not alone as I've discovered, by peeking into the nighttime windows of fiction too, of stories written by the likes of Dorothy Sayers and a host of other mystery writers who used the dark to alarm their readers until the lights come on and along with the clues everyone takes a deep breath and before long all is resolved by the friendly detective who looks like your favorite uncle. Light has been a great tool of writers everywhere.

There is a house behind me with a huge plate-glass window, and as it happens, I can see them in their nighttime window from my own bedroom window. Please know straight away that I don't look at them on purpose. It's not that I'm straining my eyes to see them there in the flickering of the television screen, but they are right there in bright lights all lit up like Picadilly Circus, and how am I supposed to close the blinds without noticing? I think they are blessed indeed to be together in their simple domestic quietude.

When I visit my daughter's house to the south of us, I like night-time drives past the colonial-style houses with gaslit lamps glowing on the porches and the brightly lit sitting rooms where I can imagine how other people's lives might take shape. Why do I care? I'm not sure.

There is a red brick house in my own city, not too far away from here, that has a huge window looking right onto the street, and they leave every light on at night. I drove by one evening in the autumn and beheld such a dinner party scenario that I wanted to knock on the door and say, "Let me in." It looked the very picture of warmth and friendship on a chilly October evening. I wondered if they recognize the gift they have in this kind of arrangement.

I like, too, to glance at the art on the walls as I drive by, the bookcases, the colors. Lime green floral wallpaper. The wingback chair beside the fireplace. Candles flickering on the sill. Perfection.

I learned this love of domestic space early on in life, I think. When my sister and I were little, our neighbor had a playhouse in their garden, built to match the style of their own home. We were allowed to play in it. It seemed such a cozy space to me, safe and lovely to imagine that we were in charge of a whole world and could do as we wished with nobody looking. My love of small over large spaces, homey versus modern, was formed then, I am sure.

The tiny cottage where I dwell now is perfect. There are diamond-paned windows that crank open and a fireplace that doesn't work, a wooden front door with an age-old nameplate on it and a blue enamel sign that announces it as Dove Cottage. Miss Marple could be quite happy in here, I believe. The front window faces east and spills over with early morning sunrise. The back window sets the scene for the sun to set in streaks across the dimming of the evening sky.

I silently wish my neighbors behind me in the big window a good night.

I repeat the words from the Sarum Primer of 1558, and I am soothed:

> "God by in my head,
> And in my understanding;
> God by in mine eyes
> And in my looking;
> God be in my mouth
> And in my speaking;
> God be in my heart,
> And in my thinking;
> God be at mine end,
> And at my departing."

Bibliography

Bakewell, Sarah. *How To Live: Or A Life of Montaigne in One Question and Twenty Attempts at an Answer*. New York: Other, 2011.

Blythe, Ronald. *Next To Nature: A Lifetime in the English Countryside*. London: John Murray, 2023.

Burton-Hill, Clemency. *Year of Wonder: Classical Music to Enjoy Day by Day*. New York: Harper, 2018.

Dickinson, Emily. *The Complete Poems of Emily Dickinson*. Edited by Thomas H. Johnson. New York: Little, Brown and Company, 1976.

Glendinning, Victoria. *Electricity: A Novel*. New York: Little, Brown and Company, 1995.

Hayden, Ruth. *Mrs. Delany: Her Life and Her Flowers*. London: British Museum, 2005.

Lee, Hermione. *Edith Wharton*. New York: Knopf, 2007.

McEntyre, Marilyn Chandler. *In Quiet Light*. Grand Rapids, MI: Wm. B. Eerdmans, 2000.

Peterson, Roger Tory. *Peterson Field Guide to the Birds of North America*. New York: Houghton Mifflin Harcourt, 2008.

Pollard Smith, Judy. "The Dam Seed Catalogue." *Hamilton Arts and Letters* (Hamilton, Ontario), April 20, 2016. https://halmagazine.wordpress.com/2016/04/20/musings-%E2%80%A2-judy-pollard-smith/

———. "I love looking into other people's lives on nighttime walks." *Globe and Mail* (Toronto, Ontario), February 5, 2024. https://www.theglobeandmail.com/life/first-person/article-i-love-looking-into-other-peoples-lives-on-nighttime-walks/

———. "The key to Edith Wharton's garden kingdom." *National Post* (Toronto, Ontario), April 4, 2015. https://nationalpost.com/opinion/judy-pollard-smith-the-key-to-edith-whartons-garden-kingdom

———. "The literary salon and how to have one." *Women Writers, Women's Books* (Publisher's Blog). Wordpress. March 12, 2015.

BIBLIOGRAPHY

Routhier, Nicole. *The Foods of Vietnam*. New York: Stewart, Tabori and Chang, 1999.

Sarton, May. *A World of Light: Portraits and Celebrations*. New York: W. W. Norton & Company, 1988.

Tan, Amy. *Backyard Bird Chronicles*. New York: Knopf, 2024.

Yeats, William Butler. *Last Poems and Two Plays*. Dublin: Cuala, 1939.

www.ingramcontent.com/pod-product-compliance
Lightning Source LLC
Chambersburg PA
CBHW072158100426
42738CB00011BA/2464